**New Directions for
Institutional Research**

Robert K. Toutkoushian
EDITOR-IN-CHIEF

J. Fredericks Volkwein
Paul D. Umbach
ASSOCIATE EDITORS

Imagining the Future of Institutional Research

Christina Leimer
EDITOR

Guan

Number 143 • Fall 2009
Jossey-Bass
San Francisco

IMAGINING THE FUTURE OF INSTITUTIONAL RESEARCH
Christina Leimer (ed.)
New Directions for Institutional Research, no. 143
Robert K. Toutkoushian, Editor-in-Chief

NEW DIRECTIONS FOR INSTITUTIONAL RESEARCH (ISSN 0271-0579, electronic ISSN 1536-075X) is part of The Jossey-Bass Higher and Adult Education Series and is published quarterly by Wiley Subscription Services, Inc., A Wiley Company, at Jossey-Bass, 989 Market Street, San Francisco, California 94103-1741 (publication number USPS 098-830). Periodicals Postage Paid at San Francisco, California, and at additional mailing offices. POSTMASTER: Send address changes to New Directions for Institutional Research, Jossey-Bass, 989 Market Street, San Francisco, California 94103-1741.

SUBSCRIPTIONS cost $109 for individuals and $264 for institutions, agencies, and libraries in the United States. See order form at end of book.

EDITORIAL CORRESPONDENCE should be sent to Robert K. Toutkoushian, Educational Leadership and Policy Studies, Education 4220, 201 N. Rose Ave., Indiana University, Bloomington, IN 47405.

New Directions for Institutional Research is indexed in *CIJE: Current Index to Journals in Education* (ERIC), *Contents Pages in Education* (T&F), and *Current Abstracts* (EBSCO).

Microfilm copies of issues and chapters are available in 16mm and 35mm, as well as microfiche in 105mm, through University Microfilms, Inc., 300 North Zeeb Road, Ann Arbor, Michigan 48106-1346.

www.josseybass.com

CONTENTS

EDITOR'S NOTES   1
Christina Leimer

1. Institutional Researchers as Change Agents   5
Randy L. Swing
Institutional research is evolving toward a unique blend of data skills, strategic planning, outcomes assessment, and advocacy for improvement. As such, institutional research professionals will be called on to act as change agents in senior leadership positions. This chapter offers suggestions for how institutional research professionals can assume this role.

2. Accountability, Accreditation, and Continuous Improvement: 17
Building a Culture of Evidence
Vanessa Smith Morest
This chapter proposes structural changes to institutional research offices, using mixed-methods research, building evaluation into new programs, and conducting research that is authentic and meaningful as ways that institutional research can play a key role in creating and sustaining a culture of evidence-based decision making and improvement.

3. Institutional Researchers' Expanding Roles: Policy, Planning,   29
Program Evaluation, Assessment, and New Research
Methodologies
Anne Marie Delaney
This chapter proposes that institutional research can exert greater influence on decision making by expanding its roles in policy development, strategic planning, assessment, accreditation, program evaluation and academic-focused research studies, and through assuming new roles such as designing programs, serving as higher education industry knowledge analysts, and functioning as knowledge brokers.

4. Laying the Foundation: Institutional Research Office   43
Organization, Staffing, and Career Development
Christina Leimer, Dawn Geronimo Terkla
Many institutional research offices are chronically understaffed. Inadequate staffing is a source of stress and job dissatisfaction for institutional research professionals. The authors discuss staffing, skills needed, hiring, training, and retaining qualified researchers. They also examine the placement of institutional research within the organization to maximize its value to the institution and higher education.

5. Increasing Demands and Changing Institutional Research   59
Roles: How Technology Can Help
Bao Huynh, Mary Frances Gibbons, Fonda Vera
A wide range of hardware and software can help institutional research
professionals meet increasing demands and changing roles. This chapter explores readily available technology that can facilitate institutional
research communication, expand its repertoire of research methods,
and ease primary data collection and reporting.

6. Raising the Institutional Research Profile: Assessing the   73
Context and Expanding the Use of Organizational Frames
Kelli A. Parmley
Institutional research is no longer just about the numbers. Getting decision makers to use data and working with faculty and external constituencies requires the ability to negotiate, collaborate, communicate,
lead, and manage people. This chapter shows institutional research professionals how they can use organizational frames, or mental models,
to develop their leadership skills, advance their careers, and gain influence for institutional research in the academy.

7. Taking a Broader View: Using Institutional Research's   85
Natural Qualities for Transformation
Christina Leimer
External pressures on higher education are pushing it toward systemic
changes that increasingly necessitate collaboration. This chapter explores some of the natural characteristics of institutional research and
its practitioners and how higher education can use them to help spur
this systemic transformation.

INDEX   95

EDITOR'S NOTES

With the demands on higher education today and in the foreseeable future, institutional research offices whose primary role is reporting and filling data requests are no longer sufficient. Requirements for continuous improvement, evidence-based decision making, and accountability require more from institutional research. In the context of shrinking budgets, where maximizing the use of limited resources is imperative, institutions must search for more efficient and effective ways of working, make decisions about which work will continue to be performed and how, and perhaps reorganize their existing programs, structures, and patterns. This too may demand more of institutional research. A decade ago, Marvin Peterson (1999) proposed that the future challenge for institutional research will be not only to help institutions improve, but to help facilitate their redesign and transformation. That time appears to have arrived. At most institutions, however, institutional research will need to redesign and transform itself to play such a substantive role.

In this volume, the chapter authors take a proactive, strategic stance by imagining the future of institutional research and how to achieve it. Taking my cue from an institutional research director whose provost asked him what the ideal institutional research office should look like, I asked the authors to respond to these questions: If you were developing an institutional research office for the next decade and you could design it any way you wanted, what would it look like? How can institutional research best serve the academy?

Many institutional research directors face these or similar questions, and some are attempting to build the future office today. To meet the increased demands on institutions, colleges and universities are creating institutional research offices, expanding existing offices, and rethinking and reshaping institutional research office responsibilities. The external climate of accountability is spurring new funding sources for institutional research (for example, the Lumina Foundation's Achieving the Dream initiative) and growing awareness of the existence and utility of institutional research (for example, the coverage by the *Chronicle of Higher Education* of the 2008 Seattle Association for Institutional Research Annual Forum). With the profession having surpassed fifty years of maturity, and a new executive director leading the Association for Institutional Research (AIR), it is an opportune time for institutional research professionals to rise to the challenges and shape our future.

In Chapter One, AIR executive director Randy Swing sees institutional research evolving toward a unique blend of data skills, strategic planning, outcomes assessment, and advocacy for improvement. In the process, institutional research professionals will become change agents in senior leadership positions. To promote this direction, he calls for action from institutional research professional associations, graduate programs, and institutional research managers and practitioners.

Vanessa Smith Morest views institutional research professionals as leaders in building a culture of evidence. In Chapter Two, she proposes making structural changes to institutional research offices using mixed-methods research, building evaluation into new programs, and conducting authentic and meaningful research as ways to develop culture.

In Chapter Three, Anne Marie Delaney contends that institutional research will increase its influence on decision making by expanding its responsibilities in policy development, strategic planning, assessment, accreditation, program evaluation, and academic-focused research studies, as well as assuming new roles such as designing programs, serving as higher education industry knowledge analysts, and functioning as knowledge brokers.

Without adequate staffing, dreams for achieving the potential of institutional research will be out of reach. In Chapter Four, Dawn Geronimo Terkla and I discuss institutional research's chronic staffing issues and ways to resolve them as part of our proposal for structuring and staffing the ideal institutional research office. Such an office would maximize the value of institutional research to the academy while offering practitioners interesting and challenging work, professional development opportunities, and career advancement.

Institutional research is technology intensive, and that emphasis is expanding along with the variety of demands being placed on institutional research offices. In Chapter Five, Bao Huynh, Mary Frances Gibbons, and Fonda Vera share their knowledge of hardware and software that can help facilitate communication, expand institutional research's methods toolbox, and lighten the data maintenance and reporting load. In addition, they remind us not to get so enamored of new technology capabilities that we fail to keep the purpose of achieving institutional goals at the forefront.

In Chapter Six, Kelli Parmley argues that institutional research is more than a numbers factory and explains why institutional research professionals need to counter that perception. Ensuring that institutional leaders use data and research to influence decision making is more likely when institutional research managers are at the table when decisions and policy are made. By developing leadership skills and raising the visibility of institutional research, college and university leaders will invite institutional research professionals to that table. Sometimes, though, institutional research professionals must take the initiative and set the table themselves.

NEW DIRECTIONS FOR INSTITUTIONAL RESEARCH • DOI: 10.1002/ir

In the final chapter, I propose that institutional research's natural tendency toward collaboration, its systems perspective, and its reputation for trustworthiness and objectivity are valuable traits that frequently operate in the limited sphere of institutional research operations. By deliberately applying those qualities more broadly in the service of institutional goals, the role of institutional research will expand, its influence will deepen, and it can play an important role in transforming higher education.

Christina Leimer
Editor

References

Basken, P. Test Touted as Two Studies Question Its Value. *Chronicle of Higher Education*, June 6, 2008, *54*(39), A1.
Glenn, D. Institutional Researchers Delve into Student Data at Annual Meeting. *Chronicle of Higher Education*, June 6, 2008, *54*(39), A24.
Peterson, M. W. "The Role of Institutional Research: From Improvement to Redesign." In J. F. Volkwein (ed.), *What Is Institutional Research All About? A Critical and Comprehensive Assessment of the Profession.* New Directions for Institutional Research, no. 104. San Francisco: Jossey-Bass, 1999.

CHRISTINA LEIMER *is director of institutional research, assessment, and planning at California State University, Fresno.*

1

The future challenge and opportunity for institutional researchers is serving as change agents. This chapter offers suggestions for how institutional researchers can become change agents and issues calls to action from institutional research professional associations, graduate programs, and managers and practitioners.

Institutional Researchers as Change Agents

Randy L. Swing

The growth in institutional computing capacity has created vast resources of data for colleges and universities. Converting those data into information for use in campus decision making has defined the work of institutional researchers for several decades. That work will continue to be the core work of institutional research, but the future of the field is already apparent in places where the institutional researcher is a full member of the president's cabinet as a senior campus leader or a senior staff member in a system office. In the future, institutional researchers will not only develop information to support decisions; they will also actively engage in the process of managing and leading institutional change. Many already are.

Contrary to the popular literature that separates leadership, management, and decision support into unique skill sets, the field of institutional research is evolving toward a unique blend of data skills, strategic planning, outcomes assessment, and advocacy for improvement. Institutional research roles historically focused primarily on the early stages of new projects, when institutions used data to define problems, and in the later stages, when institutions used data to evaluate results. Colleges and universities often leave the gap between problem definition and evaluation, the implementation phase, for others to conduct. In such an arrangement, institutional researchers should not be surprised to find that the project they must evaluate has morphed into something very different from what leaders originally conceived. Successful institutional researchers develop ongoing consultancies with strategically important campus activities.

NEW DIRECTIONS FOR INSTITUTIONAL RESEARCH, no. 143, Fall 2009 © Wiley Periodicals, Inc.
Published online in Wiley InterScience (www.interscience.wiley.com) • DOI: 10.1002/ir.301

The future challenge and opportunity for institutional researchers is to serve as change agents with involvement in initiating, implementing, and evaluating campus work. Institutional researchers are poised to excel at doing so because of the array of technical skills they routinely apply to existing institutional research roles. Their work introduces them broadly to campus systems and divisional cultures and requires them to develop critical thinking and reasoning skills that are highly transferable to an array of settings and situations. Terenzini (1999) highlighted these skills in his description of institutional research work as technical and analytical intelligence, issues intelligence, and contextual intelligence.

Fincher (1987) studied the combination of technical competencies and human skills that support successful college presidents. His analysis of the literature found that successful presidents need technical skills, such as budget management, along with behavioral and personal traits that undergird their management of people and processes. Fincher, an early leader in institutional research, could have applied his observations to the field of institutional research as well. Institutional researchers who hold senior leadership positions must have more than technical and data skills to flourish. The position announcements for directors of institutional research offices that appear on the jobs page of the Association for Institutional Research (AIR) clearly recognize the need for these skills. The idea that institutional research is a combination of technical and management skills is certainly not new. However, on many campuses, institutional research is still a relatively low-status reporting function that fails to engage fully the change advocacy role the office could provide. Campus and system offices cannot afford to waste such talent.

There are plenty of models of change management that we can apply to the role of institutional researcher. For example, the tipping point theory (Gladwell, 2000) is about the power of little things to add up. Think about a large, heavy pole standing on end. As long as the pole is balanced straight up, it takes very little energy to correct it if it should lean slightly in any direction. The amount of energy needed to push the pole back to the center balanced position increases if individuals do not take corrective action before the pole is significantly off balance. If it leans too far, eventually the weight of the out-of-balance pole is too heavy to push back into the upright position. Managing tipping points means using data to track when things start to be off balance, perhaps noting slight shifts that are not immediately obvious to casual observers, and taking action sooner rather than later. Ideally we might even predict how future winds will push us out of a balanced position. The lesson of the tipping point is to connect monitoring and corrective action. Successful change agents know that keeping effective processes working requires constant minor adjustments. Waiting until the pole is leaning enough that everyone notices its tilt (and there is consensus that we have a problem) is too late for minor adjustments to work. Institutional researchers who supply dashboard monitoring systems and oversee comparative data reporting are already using the core idea of the tipping point theory and serving a key role in change management.

Another frequently cited management guide is Jim Collins's book *Good to Great* (2001). Collins uses the metaphor of a flywheel to explain change as a process. He notes that starting a flywheel that is at rest takes a great deal of initial energy. In the early part of the process, it is easy to stop forward movement by applying brakes or drag to the flywheel or failing to continue to energize the flywheel. But once momentum develops, applying additional energy to the flywheel produces greater gains in speed with less and less effort. The result is that it becomes increasingly difficult to stop the flywheel from spinning because forward momentum is a powerful force. Collins's message is that it takes constant energy applied to the flywheel over a sustained period of time before momentum takes hold. The lesson of *Good to Great* is that change agency work requires frequent attention and the continuing application of energy, especially until change achieves some momentum. It is not enough for institutional researchers to give the flywheel a push with one round of data analysis and then hope it continues on its own.

While the perspectives of Gladwell, Collins, and other management consultants are useful for reenvisioning institutional research, they tend to treat change agency as just another aspect of leadership theory. Certainly change agents are leaders, but is there a nuanced role for institutional researchers that has yet to be defined? Have new technologies and increased data availability redefined the technical skills needed to lead change in higher education? Could institutional researchers set the stage for new theories of change management that effectively blend data and management of change processes?

The following section highlights steps in change management and the roles that institutional researchers could play in each step. I contend that in the future, colleges and universities will expect institutional researchers to bring their unique set of technical and data skills, matched with personal traits and management skills, to position themselves as senior campus leaders and change managers.

Envisioning Institutional Researchers as Change Agents

Effective change agency assumes an understanding of the predictable patterns in the adoption of new ideas and how these occur within a specific organization. Understanding these patterns allows leaders to guide others through the change process and to maximize the potential for leaders to accomplish a change successfully. I see five steps as the change paradigm in higher education. The steps provide a basic framework for how a new initiative moves from conception to integration. Each step includes opportunities for the institutional researcher serving as an agent of change.

NEW DIRECTIONS FOR INSTITUTIONAL RESEARCH • DOI: 10.1002/ir

Step 1: Build Awareness. There are many administrative stories about leaders who created organizational change on the sly. Institutional researchers may be tempted to work secretly as a strategy for changing an organization by sidestepping resistance through a surprise attack. Such a strategy may work, but it is likely to create a backlash of ill will that many will long remember and will likely create a roadblock for future change efforts. Successful change agents understand that trust is their most important personal asset and work unfailingly to establish and maintain the trust of all campus stakeholders. When leaders spring changes, those affected rarely welcome the surprises. Creating a planned strategy for building awareness of issues that a campus should address—either new opportunities or needed change—should be part of the skill set of every institutional research officer.

Rather than launching a sneak attack, institutional researchers can participate in a process of developing awareness (Ruben, 2008) to bring issues to the attention of appropriate campus constituencies. Many campuses conduct the process of awareness building as a partnership between institutional researchers and other campus leaders, beginning with the institutional researcher's becoming aware of opportunities or problems that a campus should or could address.

A common way that awareness arises is that an institutional researcher hears a hypothesis or observation put forth by a faculty member, administrator, or student. In a loosely coupled organization (Cohen and March, 1974), such as higher education, those most directly connected with students and educational processes may be the first to notice the possibility of a correlation or cause-and-effect relationship. Another common way is that an institutional researcher independently notices an issue while producing annual reports, campus fact books, dashboard monitoring systems, or peer comparisons. Whether data cause the initial awareness or confirm a casual observation, ultimately campuses should complete research and solid data analysis before publicly advancing any issue. The campus community expects institutional researchers to check the facts before making public statements and gives only limited forgiveness for crying wolf before they begin to lose trust in the institutional researcher. Institutional researchers must do their homework and avoid false alerts. They can use institutional research resources such as research journals, formal and informal networks, and data-sharing collaborations to learn what others already know that could be relevant to the situation.

Of equal importance is the role of institutional research in testing and debunking myths and false hypotheses. What may appear as intuitively obvious is often not so when rigorously examined. For example, I consulted with a campus that was convinced that it had a serious retention problem for sophomores because of a high transfer rate during the sophomore year. Detailed examination of the records showed that low grades earned in the first semester prevented students from transferring to competing state institutions until they improved their grade point average or earned additional credits. The sophomore transfer rate, which many believed was the problem, was actually only an artifact from significant issues in the first-year experiences of students. This campus made plans for several new sophomore initiatives when investment in the first year was what they needed. Debunking a widely held myth set the stage to build awareness about the real challenge facing the campus.

Of course, building awareness requires more than telling. Every institutional researcher encounters frustrating instances when campus constituents ignore data. The data do not speak for themselves. Institutional researchers must consider data to be only part of the strategy for building awareness that includes these key tasks:

Establishing a common language. Educational jargon and vaguely defined concepts are often a hindrance in building awareness of issues. It is essential to define terms because many educational concepts have very different meanings across disciplines.

Anticipating the scale and scope of awareness needed to advance the issue. Contingency theory (Fiedler, 1967) holds that what works in organizational change is situational—that is, what works in one situation may not work in another. The scale and scope of awareness needed for a successful change to take place may require the attention of a majority of the campus or might be possible with the awareness of a small number of early adopters (Rogers, 1995). Scale the awareness campaign appropriately.

Ensuring that constituents perceive the planned change as one that the campus can influence or has direct control over. Nothing is more stifling to change than the victim mentality that a problem is caused by outside forces (parents, the economy, high schools) that the campus has no ability to influence. Many understand that universities have authority over some issues, such as course scheduling, advising, or teaching methods, each of which can affect student retention and graduation. Yet it is difficult to understand more complex issues, such as budgetary allocations, without fully understanding the decision context that encompasses internal issues along with some external concerns. For instance, in public universities, states award a portion of the cost of providing education to institutions. Institutions may attempt to influence the amount of the allocation, but ultimately they must live with the final appropriation. Apportioning and use of the state funds received involves internal decisions that the institution controls. In times of shortfall, some units may attempt to conduct business as usual, seeing themselves as victims, rather than modifying the programs, methods, or types of work being done. Showing the variability of responses across campus units often demonstrates that things "don't have to be that way" and that some campus units already have altered what seemed like inevitable conditions.

Considering human desires to change. Schlesinger et al. (1979) propose that change fails because of parochial self-interest, misunderstanding due to inadequate information, low tolerance for change, and different assessments of the situation. Campuses have not completed awareness building until they have adequately addressed each of these challenges.

Especially in times of perceived urgency to change, it is tempting to shortcut the process of awareness building. Educators live in an information-rich environment with considerable competition for their attention. To overcome these challenges, change agents can meaningfully draw from a wide range of disciplinary fields including human psychology, marketing, management, and communications, as they develop skills in building awareness of issues in a campus setting. Data skills alone are unlikely to succeed. Partnering with disciplinary experts can add skills and knowledge for gaining awareness in ways that set up success.

Step 2: Develop Focus. The second step in leading institutional change is to develop focus. General awareness is necessary but insufficient to move individuals to action. In essence, focus is an enhanced awareness that establishes a fuller context of the problem or change opportunity. When focus is achieved, key stakeholders begin to develop more than a mere cursory understanding of the scale, scope, time, space, trend, and potential impact of an issue on individuals, units, and the larger organization.

Framing theory (Kahneman and Tversky, 1979) suggests that how individuals present something influences the way people think about an issue. A frame is an abstract construct that organizes and provides context for an issue. Framing issues poorly can appear to be manipulative and is intellectually insulting.

Little is more harmful to building trust than poorly framed initiatives that pit a useful change against an obviously flawed alternative as a thinly veiled attempt to control debate and move to a quick (and seemingly predetermined) conclusion. Yet framing, when done correctly, is important in moving individuals to consensus for change. In essence, framing is moving beyond just presenting the facts to presenting the facts in a context that helpfully defines issues and makes understanding complex phenomena easier. Mastering the process of framing issues, with high reliance on data-based information, is a skill that institutional researchers must master if they are to be successful in leading change. For change agents, framing is not manipulative or a process to artificially limit choice but rather a purposeful process for focusing awareness.

In an ideal world, change would rise from introspection and data analyses. In reality, awareness often follows negative events that force our attention on issues we would rather not have to address. Even a cursory review of the history of higher education reveals the regularity with which reform follows crisis. Crimes, riots, fires, scandals, financial crises, strikes, legation, resignations, and failed reaccreditation attempts certainly provide opportunities to focus awareness on college campuses. Leading change during or immediately following a period of crisis requires the discipline not to short-change the processes in awareness building or the process of adequately establishing focus. What follow are key tasks in building focus for change:

Communicating data-based information that identifies and disaggregates components of complex issues. Particularly important is communication that does not confuse problems with potential solutions. Many begin debating solutions well before they fully understand the issues.

Continue (from awareness building) refining the language used in defining issues. After building initial awareness, there is strong temptation to assume that everyone understands the issues and agrees on short names for constructs. It is too easy to lose focus if linguistic confusion develops.

Ensuring that others can articulate the timeliness of issues. It is important to answer the question, "Why change now?"

Communicating what is not within the scope of the issue of reference. Without establishing limits, problems or opportunities can become so large that addressing them appears to be hopeless.

Encouraging debate and discussion of the issues. (Avoid moving too quickly to debating solutions.) The natural strengths of academics are questioning and debating. Embrace and encourage meaningful discourse. Asking dissenters to propose a change, "How would you fix this?" may be more useful than defending a particular plan of action.

A successful focus effort limits the scope of a potential change to the most important portion. Researchers such as Julius, Baldridge, and Pfeffer (2000) suggest that "subsidiary processes"—the piling on of related change initiatives that result in a loss of focus—can easily overwhelm change efforts.

Step 3: Increase Knowledge. Awareness and focus center on defining issues that might be changed. The next step is increasing knowledge that campuses will need for understanding identified issues and evaluating potential solutions and opportunities. It is an interesting irony that academics who rely on theory and prior research in their own scholarship so quickly abandon those habits of mind when approaching administrative tasks. In developing new courses and programs, academics often decide to go it alone rather than research how others are dealing with the same or similar issues (Swing, 1998). Institutional researchers should set the example by identifying relevant research and providing information from peer institutions or systems.

Fortunately, the institutional research community is a network of professionals who enjoy sharing and have established a number of formal and informal structures for doing so. Using peer comparisons and benchmarks can increase an organization's knowledge base. Data sharing consortia and the Integrated Postsecondary Education Data System are natural means of locating comparable data and are tools often used by institutional researchers but perhaps unknown to most faculty, staff, and other administrators.

Finding aspirational peers, institutions that are already performing at enviable levels, may be a first step in identifying potential solutions. Literature reviews, attending conferences, reading case studies, and formal and informal networking have the potential to increase campus knowledge of ways to address an identified issue that needs to change. It is not enough just to identify problems or opportunities. The goal in the knowledge-building phase is to deepen the understanding of an issue a campus has identified as needing improvement and to assist decision makers and stakeholders in weighing potential solutions.

After the goal of the knowledge-building phase is successfully achieved, a critical mass of stakeholders will be able to identify one or more potential changes that could address the identified problem (or opportunity). In addition, those individuals should be able to explain how the change effort will create positive outcomes.

Because this step is so critical to the long-term success of the change process, it is worth sampling stakeholders to test their understanding of the issues and knowledge of the proposed change. One test of a group's understanding of a potential change initiative is to ask them to develop outcome measures that will prove in the future if the change was successful. Writing outcomes demands a clear understanding of processes, the interconnections among processes, and agreement on the desired results after a campus fully implements change. Key tasks include using peer comparisons to identify aspirational peers and those who have dealt with the same issue and seen positive outcomes, using reference sources to identify potential solutions, developing understanding of how the proposed change will result in positive outcomes, and identifying outcomes that will define success.

The result of knowledge building is to move the campus from considering the problem or opportunity broadly to a narrowing of potential actions. By the end of this stage of change, consensus about next steps should be apparent.

Step 4: Resolve to Change. It is naive to believe that organizations will embrace change even if it is clearly in the best interest of the majority. Julius, Baldridge, and Pfeffer (2000) argue that the very idea of decision making in higher education is a delusion. They use the phrase *decision flow* to describe the decision-making process in higher education and explain that after colleges and universities make decisions, they can readily be reversed or diverted during execution or fade over time. Resolving to change is not unlike best-intentioned New Year resolutions that often fail to stick. Individuals need resolve to continue pushing the flywheel to build momentum (Collins, 2001).

Of course, there are myriad theories of human behavior and motivation leaders could use to improve the success of change initiatives, but managing change often involves juggling varied and even conflicting motivations. Contingency theory (Fiedler, 1967) holds that successful strategies are highly situational. What works in some situations may not work well in others. Using pilot projects and small-scale demonstration programs and sharing case studies from other successful organizations are tools to build and maintain resolve.

Institutional researchers with long experience on a campus gain organizational knowledge that helps them understand political alignments and engage appropriate power brokers in change initiatives. Nevertheless, leading change is not just for the wise long marchers. Institutional researchers who lack long histories with their current institution can partner with experienced faculty and staff in planning and developing institutional engagement in change. In fact, institutional researchers are often consultants to committees, and in that role, they can advise that change plans include clear time lines, individuals responsible for each aspect of future steps, rewards for those who cooperate and participate, and consequences if the initiative is not initiated.

There are several key tasks for building and maintaining the resolve to change. First, it is important to understand campus dynamics and history that support or oppose the recommended change. Second, leaders should disseminate and clearly communicate the change plan. Third, institutional researchers can assist decision makers in establishing and monitoring a time line, identifying and consulting with responsible parties, and establishing rewards and consequences. Finally, campuses should track change processes across initiation, implementation, and continuation phases.

Following up is essential to keep change efforts on track as intended. Such efforts include monitoring outcomes and early indicators of intended outcomes. Institutional researchers are in a unique position to use results from dashboards, data reports, and other forms of institutional information to renew and refocus campus resolve when a change process stops producing the desired results.

Step 5: Incorporate or Replace. It is highly satisfying to initiate change successfully, especially if that change proves to be a true improvement over prior performance. Understanding, however, that change is an ongoing process—a journey and not a destination—it is essential that campuses subject change initiatives to evaluation and scrutiny over time. It is quite likely that a successful change will alter other aspects of the campus in ways that may even make the initial change less important or counterproductive. Unintended consequences also can invalidate processes that were initially successful.

"Even the new ideas that you worked so hard to establish will, in time, be dull and old" is the observation of Julius, Baldridge, and Pfeffer (2000, p. 58). They conclude that the most difficult skill of a change agent may be to "kill your own projects when they have outlived their usefulness" (p. 58). Fairly evaluating efforts (of your own making as well as those conceived by others) is difficult, but it is essential in building and maintaining the trust of campus constituencies. Institutional researchers must know when to seek peer review of their work or even to outsource evaluation to neutral parties. The appearance of spinning data for one's own self-interest will serve only to produce long-ranging negative consequences for change agents.

For changes that do prove successful, the work is not finished until the appropriate constituencies properly vet the processes and formalize them within organizational structures. Examples of institutionalizing new processes include budgeting and resource allocations, staffing, inclusion in written procedures, alignment with organizational evaluation, promotion, reward structures, and embedding elements in the organization's strategic planning cycles.

The goal is not to make the change so fixed that a campus cannot reverse, but rather to ensure that it will continue as a normal procedure that is subject to intentional revision and continuous improvement. The key to success is building a leadership succession plan into new initiatives from the beginning. Case studies show that good processes often disappear when key advocates leave leadership positions (Barefoot and others, 2005). Planning for smooth transitions is essential for creating lasting change but too often is an afterthought in the planning process. Institutional researchers, as consultants in change planning, should raise questions about leadership, formalizing change initiates, and embedding change in existing structures.

Developing Institutional Research Capacity

A rich literature describes good practices for managing change using formal administrative authority. Advice includes how to appoint the right kinds of people to serve in key roles, how to provide rewards to those who advance the cause, and how to control difficult people—meaning anyone who does not agree with the proposed change. The literature is not as deep about how to be a change agent without formal authority to appoint, reward, and control others. Yet there are myriad opportunities to support change efforts that do not require formal power. Many fruitful change support strategies align with the skills that institutional researchers already use in their daily work. Others seem to be natural extensions of the traits that good institutional researchers bring to their jobs. Still, institutional researchers who wish to master the process of change agency could learn other skills.

Perhaps the most critical missing part is that many institutional researchers have established their own fences around their position. Some wear the phrase "just report the facts" as a badge of honor. But just reporting the facts often fails to carry change through to full institutionalization and understates the skills and talents that institutional research could bring to improving postsecondary education. The first step in helping institutional research officers find their role as agents of change is to make that role part of the self-perceptions and expectations that institutional research officers bring to their assignments. The call to action is to ensure that institutional researchers see statistical analysis as only one step in their role of decision support. Initiation, building support for, implementing, and institutionalizing change are all natural extensions of the work already assigned to the institutional research office.

Some institutional researchers already have the skills to perform successfully as change agents, but many do not. The call to action for graduate degree programs in higher education and institutional research certificate programs is to develop a course in change management for postsecondary education settings. Such a course would be interdisciplinary, drawing on concepts from psychology, management, political science, leadership studies, adult education, human resource management, evaluation, and others. Programs should exercise caution that a semester of old war stories might prove more satisfying to the instructor than useful to the student. A course in change advocacy, built on theory and including case examples, should provide students a working base for their first employment in institutional research.

Directors of institutional research units also have a call to action. They should work with staff members to create professional development plans that include opportunities to follow projects from concept to implementation. In addition to workshops and conferences that enhance technical skills, each professional development plan should include opportunities to cultivate personal skills such as listening, consulting, developing useful framing and communications strategies, and understanding human motivations. Directors should expect clear writing and provide opportunities for staff to practice oral communications within the institutional research unit to build confidence and skills. Most important, annual evaluations should reward growth in technical and personal skills that reflect the skills needed to participate fully in organizational change in postsecondary education settings. Even the least experienced staff member should find that the institutional research office is a place that demands accuracy, never jeopardizes trust, expects researchers to put data in a useful context, avoids educational jargon and shorthand names that cause confusion, and thinks across the steps in implementing change.

Institutional research professional associations have a call to action to meet the training needs of institutional research officers. Associations should provide opportunities for participants to develop the skills needed to be change agents and should offer networking opportunities that allow the exchange of ideas about strategies that work.

While there are multiple opportunities to help institutional researchers develop their skills, the most important first step is for institutional research officers to expand their own thinking about their role in the academy. It is not necessary to hang a new sign on the institutional research office that proclaims that "the change agent is in." Rather, institutional research officers can earn the role by applying the skills they already have to the process of organizational change. The most successful change agents may hardly be recognized as such. It is, however, unlikely that successful senior campus leaders will fail to notice or appreciate that institutional research, when performed well, can help them reach their goals as leaders too.

References

Barefoot, B. O., and others. *Achieving and Sustaining Institutional Excellence for the First Year of College.* San Francisco: Jossey-Bass, 2005.

Cohen, M. D., and March, J. G. *Leadership and Ambiguity: The American College President.* Boston: Harvard Business School Press, 1974.

Collins, J. *Good to Great: Why Some Companies Make the Leap—and Others Don't.* New York: HarperBusiness, 2001.

Fiedler, F. E. *A Theory of Leadership Effectiveness.* New York: McGraw-Hill, 1967.

Fincher, C. "Personal Qualities and Role Behavior in Presidential Leadership." Paper presented at the annual meeting of the Association for the Study of Higher Education, San Diego, Calif., 1987.

Gladwell, M. *The Tipping Point: How Little Things Can Make a Big Difference.* New York: Little, Brown, 2000.

Julius, D. J., Baldridge, V., and Pfeffer, J. "A Memorandum from Machiavelli on the Principled Use of Power in the Academy." In A. M. Hoffman and R. W. Summers (eds.), *Managing Colleges and Universities: Issues for Leadership.* Westport, Conn.: Bergin and Garvey, 2000.

Kahneman, D., and Tversky, A. "Prospect Theory: An Analysis of Decision Under Risk." *Econometrica,* 1979, 47(2), 263–291.

Rogers, E. M. *Diffusion of Innovation.* New York: Free Press, 1995.

Ruben, B. D. "Understanding, Leading and Planning Social and Organizational Change." In B. Ruben, D. L. Lewis, and L. Sandmeyer (eds.), *Assessing the Impact of the Spellings Commission.* Washington, D.C.: NACUBO, 2008.

Schlesinger, P. F., Schlesinger, L. A., Sathe, V., and Kotter, J. P. *Organization: Text, Cases, and Readings on the Management of Organization Design and Change.* Homewood, Ill.: Irwin, 1979.

Swing, R. L. "A Case Study of New Course Development in Higher Education." Unpublished doctoral dissertation, University of Georgia, 1998.

Terenzini, P. T. "On the Nature of Institutional Research and the Knowledge and Skills It Requires." In J. F. Volkwein (ed.), *What Is Institutional Research All About? A Critical and Comprehensive Assessment of the Profession.* New Directions for Institutional Research, no. 104. San Francisco: Jossey-Bass, 1999.

Randy L. Swing is executive director of the Association for Institutional Research, Tallahassee, Florida.

2

Using mixed methods, building evaluation into new programs, and conducting research that is authentic and meaningful to the internal campus community can generate interest and help fuel a data-intensive cultural transformation.

Accountability, Accreditation, and Continuous Improvement: Building a Culture of Evidence

Vanessa Smith Morest

Like other public sector institutions, higher education has become part of the accountability movement. Colleges and universities increasingly rely on institutional research offices to document performance by providing data to external audiences. In fact, most of the funding available to colleges and universities today comes with some kind of reporting requirement. In addition, accrediting bodies have significantly shifted their orientation toward data-driven continuous improvement. These two forces have thrust institutional research offices into the spotlight.

From the standpoint of institutional researchers, this attention is both exciting and bewildering, particularly in smaller colleges and institutions with limited institutional research capacity. These developments are exciting in that there is greater demand for research and data. Furthermore, as institutional research becomes integrated into strategic planning and assessment, it is increasingly a core administrative function. But most institutional research offices lack the capacity to evaluate institution-wide everything from student learning outcomes to retention and graduation. Even more complicated and demanding is the expectation of cultural change—that faculty, staff, and administrators will rely on hard evidence to guide institutional policy and practice.

New Directions for Institutional Research, no. 143, Fall 2009 © Wiley Periodicals, Inc.
Published online in Wiley InterScience (www.interscience.wiley.com) • DOI: 10.1002/ir.302

17

Organizational theorists describe accountability pressures as external to the organization (Scott, 2002). This means that they are beyond institutional control, and yet they exert considerable influence over internal operations. External pressures do not consistently push institutions in a single direction, and at times these pressures are in conflict with one another. This is true of the conflicting pressures of mandatory reporting and accreditation. The data that colleges and universities report to federal and state governments are different from those that these institutions collect and analyze for the purpose of systematic assessment for accreditation. This is just one challenge confronting institutional research offices as they play their role in contributing to a culture of evidence.

This chapter focuses on the challenges and possibilities of building a culture of evidence. I begin with some discussion of the background of this movement. Changing institutional culture is a complex undertaking, and this particular request for change calls for the development of an array of new processes and structures. Motivating faculty and staff to engage in institutional transformation by contributing to and supporting institutional research and assessment in their daily practice is the challenge facing many college administrators. I believe that the key to overcoming these challenges lies in recognizing that the constituents of institutional research offices are internal, rather than external, stakeholders of the organization. Faculty, staff, and administrators will pay attention to and support research that is authentic and meaningful to them.

What Is a Culture of Evidence?

The phrase *culture of evidence* is popular among policy and assessment experts. It captures the belief that colleges can enhance student learning and success if they systematically collect and examine data. Underlying this insight, however, is an assumption that colleges typically make decisions without the benefit of data. This interpretation of the problem does not take into consideration that many postsecondary institutions do collect and analyze data in certain functional areas. For example, selective colleges scrutinize admissions data, just as community colleges look for trends in enrollment data. Furthermore, colleges and universities devote extensive time and resources to self-studies for accreditation and collect data for program review. The problem therefore is not so much the absence of data as the focus of data collection and the data sources and methodologies researchers employ.

A second factor in considering data use in higher education is that it is not always clear when and where postsecondary institutions make decisions. Which decisions should be based on empirical evidence, and what kinds of evidence are acceptable? Individuals and groups at every level of the institution constantly make decisions, whether it is a decision to give an A or a B when grading a student's paper or to expand a scholarship program. In the case of formal decisions that require resources, these decisions may take months or years to wend their way through the organizational decision-making process. Where public institutions are concerned, legislatures, state offices, and other entities often pass down policy decisions that are well beyond the control of the institutions.

Sociologists have studied how public educational institutions use data. Meyer and Rowan (1977) identified public postsecondary institutions as possessing organizational structures that preserve the legitimacy of their functions to the outside world. Their theory of institutionalization provides some useful insights into the culture of evidence in postsecondary education. First, institutions are likely to focus on generating data and information that will strengthen the status of the institution. Using the earlier example, open access institutions can demonstrate their accessibility by reporting on enrollment growth. Second, the primary focus of institutional research is to satisfy the demands of an external, as opposed to internal, audience that includes a long list of stakeholders, including policymakers, legislators, taxpayers, system offices, and trustees.

Studies suggest that institutional research offices devote many of their resources to compiling data for compliance reporting purposes. Often it is the mandatory reporting that institutional researchers identify as taking up much of their time (Morest and Jenkins, 2007). Some of these reporting requirements include providing data for the federal Integrated Postsecondary Data System data collection, reporting for state and federal grants or state departments of higher education, and updating institutional records such as fact books. These are considered to be the administrative functions of institutional research offices. Establishing a culture of evidence recasts the role of institutional research as providing data for internal functioning and satisfying external mandates.

The shift toward evidence entails a focus on outcomes. For example, a report published by the Educational Testing Service (ETS) states: "Postsecondary education today is not driven by hard evidence of its effectiveness. Consequently, our current state of knowledge about the effectiveness of a college education is limited. The lack of a culture oriented toward evidence of specific student outcomes hampers informed decision-making by institutions, by students and their families, and by the future employers of college graduates" (Dwyer, Millett, and Payne, 2006, p. 1).

Whether we agree with this kind of commentary, it is clear that institutional reform around a culture of evidence relies on the idea that data collection and analysis should be extensive and systematic. The ideal would be for diagnostic information to be available to every stakeholder of the institution, including students, faculty, administrators, and future employers. Petrides (2004) defines this culture as one "that purposefully reflects on its own practices and then proactively creates and implements actions that respond to organizational problems or issues" (p. 45). Dowd (2005) expands on this concept by calling for a culture of inquiry—"one in which data move out of the limelight, and practitioners move to center stage" (p. 1).

Developing a culture of evidence therefore calls for organizational change in multiple areas. It requires that actors at all levels of the organization collect and use data to inform their practice. In order to accomplish this, constituents must perceive the data as relevant. The relevance of data is a matter of perception because faculty, staff, and administrators all have different needs and interests (Romero, Purdy, Rodriguez, and Richards, 2005). Once campus groups and leaders make data readily available, actors within the institution must be prepared to do something with the information. The institution must be sure to build in mechanisms through which data and research can help determine policies and practice.

Practical Implications of an Expanded Role for Research

Research methods for a culture of evidence are more resource intensive than the data required for mandatory external reporting. When an institution moves toward a culture of evidence, campuses ask institutional research offices to accept broad new responsibilities. There has been little discussion in the literature about the implications or consequences of a culture of evidence and the ability of institutional research offices to respond to this shift in culture. Furthermore, the research that does exist indicates that institutional research offices suffer from underfunding even before undertaking an expansion of their role (Harrington, Christie, and Chen, 1996; Morest and Jenkins, 2007).

A major national grant program that is providing some feedback on building a culture of evidence is the Achieving the Dream: Community Colleges Count initiative, launched by the Lumina Foundation in 2003. The initiative operates in four areas—institutional change, policy change, public engagement, and knowledge development—with the goal of increasing student success, particularly for low-income students and students of color. The foundation requires the colleges selected to participate in the initiative to "use data to identify problems, set goals, establish institutional priorities, allocate resources and measure progress" (Achieving the Dream, 2005). Through this initiative, over eighty community colleges in fifteen states are working to develop a culture of evidence.

The National Evaluation of Achieving the Dream found that among the first twenty-seven community colleges to participate, the "most common obstacle to building a culture of evidence is the difficulty many colleges have retrieving and analyzing data" (Brock and others, 2007, p. 38). Their difficulties stemmed from two sources: information technology, which provides only limited or overly complicated access to data, and a shortage of institutional research staff. These results are consistent with other studies. For example, in a national survey of community college institutional researchers, we learned that 86 percent reported the need for additional staff as necessary to improve their operations and 56 percent sought additional professional development for staff. By contrast, less than a third sought more competitive pay, hardware or software improvements, or increased support from senior administrators (Morest and others, 2006).

The first step toward establishing a culture of evidence ought to begin with a logistical discussion about the degree to which resources are available to undertake this kind of organizational change. Institutions need to give attention to the practical foundations of expanding and diversifying data collection and use. Specifically, does the institution possess the resources required to undertake a data-intensive cultural transformation?

Data Organization and Accessibility. The student information system is the primary repository of institutional data that institutional researchers can translate into research and analyses. These systems contain the full range of records of student enrollment, course taking, financial aid, and family background. They have mechanisms to allow data entry by the many faculty and staff who come into contact with each student. Student information systems are structured to facilitate data entry and pulling individual student records. They are less well equipped for extracting data for research purposes.

In order to cope with this problem, some states and colleges have moved toward data warehouses or business intelligence systems. These differ in their functionality; however, in both cases, they are information technology add-ons that improve access to data that researchers can use. In order to begin to develop a culture of evidence, it is essential that institutional research offices are able to access data quickly and reliably. Speed of access has to do with the availability of reports and the degree to which the institutions have organized data around the types of questions being asked of researchers. For instance, if an institution is concerned about retention rates of low-income students, to what extent can institutional researchers easily identify these students in the data? Reliability becomes an issue when data definitions are not clear. In the preceding example, it would be important to have agreed-on definitions for *retention* and *low income*.

A failure to assess the ease of access to institutional data accurately can create problems for an institution seeking to develop a culture of evidence. The National Evaluation of Achieving the Dream colleges found that the project suddenly thrust institutional researchers into the middle of college decision making, and these researchers were overwhelmed by requests for data (Brock and others, 2007). In addition, without consistency in definitions, and when data extracted from the student information system require significant manipulation before researchers can use them, the chances of making a mistake increase.

Institutional Research Staff. In our study of institutional research offices at community colleges, we found that nearly three-quarters of the colleges surveyed had two or fewer full-time equivalent institutional research staff, and just over half had less than one full-time equivalent (Morest and Jenkins, 2007). In fact, nearly 20 percent of the colleges surveyed had less than a full-time position devoted to institutional research. Conducting research with the expectation of learning about student outcomes requires a considerable investment of time because it means, at a minimum, tracking students longitudinally. The time demands placed on institutional research offices that are contributing to cultural change are great because they require much more active and public participation in the institution, frequent report writing, and a wider range of research methods. Institutions undertaking cultural change therefore must consider whether their current institutional research staff can handle the increased demand for data in terms of both person-hours and the knowledge set and background experiences of the institutional research staff.

Investing resources to improve data access will also increase the research capacity of institutional research staff. If an institution can reduce the time that researchers spend obtaining and organizing data, researchers can reinvest their time in expanding the institution's research agenda. Improved ease of access to data also means that institutional researchers can delegate certain tasks to research assistants or individuals with limited training or experience in research. Another way to maximize the capacity of institutional researchers is to automate reporting functions and centralize mandatory external reporting to the system level in the case of public postsecondary institutions. Finally, because it is unlikely that institutions will have sufficient research capacity to satisfy the requests of all college constituents, campuses must consider the capacity of institutional research staff in the prioritization of research questions and the selection of outcome indicators (Alfred, Shults, and Seybert, 2007).

Organizational Structure. A third practical consideration involves the location of institutional research within the institution. Campuses situate institutional research offices in a variety of organizational locations. Many times they report to academic affairs, but they may also report to a department of research and planning or institutional advancement. Because developing a culture of evidence requires an institution-wide investment in research, it makes sense to position the research department in such a way that the functional area does not overly influence the department's goals. In addition, placing a senior administrator in charge of research ensures that the university or college president is directly involved and that an individual with knowledge of the research findings is present at the table for high-level meetings and planning sessions. Research suggests that the seniority of institutional researchers is critical to their efficacy in influencing institutional policymaking (Delaney, 2001). For instance, studies have indicated that institutional researchers holding doctorates are more involved in policymaking and perceive themselves to be more effective in having an impact on institutional policy (Delaney, 2001; Knight, Moore, and Coperthwaite, 1997).

The positioning of institutional research and the leadership qualities of institutional research directors begin to deal with the problem of changing institutional culture. Even if an institution has successfully managed the logistics of increasing capacity to satisfy the demand for data and research, actors in the institution may not engage in change. Engaging faculty and staff in seeking out and using evidence as part of their daily practice requires that they perceive the process as valuable and a productive use of their time.

Building a Culture of Evidence

I began this chapter by describing some of the external factors motivating a movement toward developing a culture of evidence within higher education. These factors are external to the institutions. In other words, external agents are mandating that colleges and universities develop student learning outcomes assessment, core indicators, and quality education plans, to name a few, in order to maintain their accreditation and receive state and federal resources. Because college administrators are responsible for organizing operations to respond to these mandates, it becomes difficult to reframe these external requests for data and research as beneficial to all actors in the institution, as opposed to primarily administrators.

My own experience as an administrator leading a new department charged with the goal of guiding a community college toward embracing a culture of evidence suggests to me that there are ways to involve a wide range of college constituents in institutional research. The results of their involvement can be productive and even empowering. A critical insight to this process is the recognition that undertaking cultural change ultimately must be a bottom-up, as opposed to top-down, decision. As long as building a culture of evidence is perceived as an external demand which has been translated into an administrative priority, college faculty, staff and even other administrators, are unlikely to see value in investing limited time and resources into institutional research. However, turning over control of the research agenda to college constituents can lead to research that is authentic and even welcomed. In this section, I describe several strategies that support this approach.

The Advantages of Using Mixed Methods. Employing both qualitative and quantitative methodologies can be highly effective for institutional researchers. Many often overlook qualitative research because it can be more time-consuming and difficult to arrange, and its results may lack the generalizability afforded by analyzing a large quantitative data set. However, qualitative research, including interviews, focus groups, and small-scale surveys, has some hidden benefits that in my experience have been very effective in building a culture of evidence.

At Norwalk Community College (NCC), we are employing formative evaluation methods on a routine basis with the development of new programs. Stakeholders use feedback from formative evaluation during the early stages of program development. This approach does not claim to provide evidence of impact or causality because a program that is newly developing has many characteristics that can interfere with an accurate assessment of its efficacy. For example, new programs or interventions may be underenrolled, or they may undergo significant revisions of the strategies employed. Institutions that use research oriented toward supporting the development of new programs and carry out the research with the direct input and involvement of faculty and staff find this approach is less threatening and more productive.

Using qualitative methodologies creates an environment where there is less distance between the researchers and their subjects, and a broad audience can easily understand the results of qualitative inquiry. The nature of qualitative research is that researchers have to interact directly with their subjects. This offers a better opportunity to explain the methodology and the purposes of the study and answer questions. In these interactions, institutional researchers have the opportunity to earn trust and interest in their work. One of the challenges of compliance reporting is that often institutional researchers do it in relative isolation from the institution. In fact, a degree of separation is desirable to ensure objectivity. However, this social distance does not help make research accessible and integrated into college functioning.

Although the research design, instrumentation, and analysis of qualitative data require a solid background in social science research, it is possible to train people without this background to collect the data. In other words, skilled qualitative researchers can train faculty, staff, or early-career research assistants to administer a survey, conduct an interview, or lead a focus group. By contrast, organizing, cleaning, and analyzing student data are far more complicated. In order to engage in statistical inference or employ an experimental design, researchers need expertise in measurement and statistics. Work that requires these advanced skills can present limitations to a director of institutional research who is seeking to delegate work to others in a small office.

Making Research an Essential Element in the Development of New Programs. Rather than adding assessment to established and institutionalized practices, an approach that has worked at NCC is to begin by focusing on new programs. There are benefits to using formative evaluation as a way to bring about cultural change. By involving a researcher from the very early stages of program development, assessment of an initiative is part of the process as opposed to an add-on that will require unplanned or unbudgeted work. For example, when researchers or administrators are writing grants, foundations and granting agencies frequently require some form of evaluation. Using the college's institutional researchers to design and execute the evaluation means that colleges can direct some of the grant's overhead toward the institutional research office, helping colleges deal with institutional research staff shortages.

Furthermore, the college can incorporate the new program's data collection and analysis efforts into the institution's system of assessment. For example, at NCC, we have a common set of indicators that we apply to different subsets of the student population. This element of the evaluation dovetails with preexisting structures at the college, which mitigates the additional workload involved in data analysis.

Over time it becomes an expectation that a researcher will be involved with program development or policy change. This is a research and development function, which many perceive as meaningful and often helpful. For example, in the development of learning communities at NCC, we were able to demonstrate very early on that fall-to-spring retention rates are high for the participating students. Furthermore, surveys indicated that students were highly satisfied with their experiences. Discussion of these findings contributed to the generation of the much needed attention and support for the program from the college's department chairs. In another instance, our institutional research office analyzed data systematically collected by mathematics and science faculty and documented students' growing awareness and participation levels in an initiative aimed at improving grades. While it is too early to tell whether the desired impact is present, we are able to show that students have come to expect and seek out the extra support offered by the faculty.

Establishing Structures to Support Institutional Research. In order for cultural change to become institutionalized, colleges need to develop new structures that support the change. Building these structures can be an intentional element of creating a culture of evidence. Some colleges have established committees for the purpose of reviewing evidence. Often these committees focus on core indicators, assessment, or strategic planning. At NCC, we have created a research advisory board that brings together individuals interested in research from across the college. The purpose of this group is to review and discuss research findings and provide feedback, which aids in the interpretation of data and the prioritization of future research. The Achieving the Dream model has a core team and a data team, with faculty, staff, and administrator members, and this diverse team approach gives them an opportunity to drive data collection and analysis.

While committee meetings offer opportunities to involve faculty and staff directly in institutional research, routine publications can touch an even broader audience. For example, newsletters that highlight recent findings with short, nontechnical descriptions can increase knowledge of institutional research activities. This can also present an opportunity for college constituents to reflect on institutional policies and practices.

Another structural change is creating opportunities for interested individuals to work temporarily in the institutional research office as interns or research assistants. For instance, graduate students recruited to participate in institutional research gain valuable research practice and experience, while at the same time increasing the capacity of the department. I have found that when graduate students have a successful experience working in institutional research, they pass the information on to others in their program, creating a potential pipeline for future graduate assistants and new institutional research practitioners. I have also recruited community college information technology students who are seeking co-op or internship experiences. We are also establishing service-learning opportunities for students whom staff will train to run focus groups.

Conclusions

Establishing a culture of evidence is an external mandate calling for institutions to report to internal audiences. Paradoxically, one of the challenges of establishing a culture of evidence appears to be creating those audiences. The reward for establishing a culture of evidence is reflective practice. In a sense, an analogy for this might be going to the doctor for a routine physical examination. It is only by weighing, measuring, and taking blood pressure and blood samples that physicians can capture trends and identify and diagnose problems. Furthermore, these data can be used to understand whether interventions are having the desired effects.

In higher education, identifying measures and methodologies that are both useful and feasible pose a major institutional challenge. The first step to engage in this challenge is to assess the institution's capacity for conducting institutional research on a larger scale. This includes uncomplicated and efficient access to data and enough research staff to take on the additional work. It also involves positioning institutional research within the organization in such a way that researchers can become leaders.

Finally, institutional research leaders need to recognize the important role that they can play in generating interest in research and assessment. In order for research to be useful to institutions, faculty, staff, and administrators must value its results. In our study, we learned that community college institutional researchers often reserved their most rigorous research for professional journals and conferences (Morest and others, 2006). The hallmarks of rigorous research—including comparison groups, longitudinal study, triangulation, and the clear acknowledgment of a study's limitations—are important to gaining the trust and respect of college constituents that will eventually lead to cultural change. A prerequisite to employing these tools is that postsecondary leaders need to support their institutional researchers by offering them the status and resources that will enable them to move research from the margins to the core of organizational functions.

References

Achieving the Dream. "Logic Model." 2005. Retrieved January 5, 2009, from http://www.achievingthedream.org/_images/_index03/LogicModelAug2005.pdf.

Alfred, R., Shults, C., and Seybert, J. *Core Indicators of Effectiveness for Community Colleges.* Washington D.C.: American Association of Community Colleges, 2007.

Brock, T., and others. *Building a Culture of Evidence for Community College Student Success: Early Progress in the Achieving the Dream Initiative.* New York: MDRC and Community College Research Center (CCRC), 2007.

Delaney, A. M. "Institutional Researchers' Perceptions of Effectiveness." *Research in Higher Education*, 2001, 42(2), 197–210.

Dowd, A. C. *Data Don't Drive: Building a Practitioner-Driven Culture of Inquiry to Assess Community College Performance.* Indianapolis: Lumina Foundation, 2005.

Dwyer, C. A., Millett, C. M., and Payne, D. G. *A Culture of Evidence: Postsecondary Assessment and Learning Outcomes.* Princeton, N.J.: Educational Testing Service (ETS), June 2006.

Harrington, C. F., Christie, R. L., and Chen, H. Y. "Does Institutional Research Really Contribute to Institutional Effectiveness: Perceptions of Institutional Research Effectiveness as Held by College and University Presidents." Paper presented at the Thirty-Sixth Annual Forum of the Association for Institutional Research, Albuquerque, New Mexico, May 5–8, 1996.

Knight, W. E., Moore, M. E., and Coperthwaite, C. A. "Institutional Research: Knowledge, Skills, and Perceptions of Effectiveness." *Research in Higher Education*, 1997, 38(4), 419–433.

Meyer, J. W., and Rowan, B. "Institutional Organizations: Formal Structure as Myth and Ceremony." *American Journal of Sociology*, 1977, 83(2), 340–63.

Morest, V. S., and Jenkins, D. *Institutional Research and the Culture of Evidence at Community Colleges.* Report No. 1 in the Achieving the Dream Culture of Evidence Series. New York: Community College Research Center, Teachers College, Columbia University, April 2007.

Morest, V. S., Soonachan, A., Reid, M., Leinbach, T., and Crosta, P. "Institutional Research in Community Colleges." Paper presented at the annual meeting of the American Educational Research Association, San Francisco, Apr. 7–11, 2006.

Petrides, L. *Turning Knowledge into Action: What's Data Got to Do with It?* Phoenix, Ariz.: League for Innovation in the Community College, 2004.

Romero, M., Purdy, L., Rodriguez, L., and Richards, S. "Research Needs and Practices of Community-College Practitioners." *Community College Journal of Research and Practice*, 2005, 29(4), 289–302.

Scott, W. R. *Organizations: Rational, Natural, and Open Systems.* (5th ed.) Upper Saddle River, N.J.: Prentice Hall, 2002.

VANESSA SMITH MOREST is dean of institutional effectiveness at Norwalk Community College in Norwalk, Connecticut.

NEW DIRECTIONS FOR INSTITUTIONAL RESEARCH • DOI: 10.1002/ir

3

This chapter explores how institutional researchers can enhance their value by expanding roles in policy, planning, evaluation and assessment, and by assuming new roles in program design and knowledge generation.

Institutional Researchers' Expanding Roles: Policy, Planning, Program Evaluation, Assessment, and New Research Methodologies

Anne Marie Delaney

Institutional researchers can best serve higher education in the twenty-first century by enhancing their current roles and adopting new roles to exert greater influence on decision making. This chapter explores how they can achieve this by expanding roles in policy development, strategic planning, assessment, accreditation, program evaluation, and academic-focused research studies. The chapter also proposes new roles for institutional researchers—designing new programs, serving as higher education industry knowledge analysts, and functioning as knowledge brokers. The crucial role of administrators, researcher qualifications required for success, and implications for institutional research offices are also discussed.

Expanded Roles in Current Areas of Institutional Research

Institutional researchers can enhance their effectiveness in policy development and strategic planning by assuming new roles, developing creative strategies, and increasing their knowledge of an institution's internal culture and external environment. To effectively influence policy, institutional researchers need to be capable policy analysts, competent debaters, and

skillful teachers. To support strategic planning, they need to be cognizant of the institution's goals and issues and skilled in two critical areas—environmental scanning and benchmarking.

Enhanced Role in Policy Development. Leaders and scholars in the profession have long recognized the importance of institutional researchers' involvement in policy. They have proposed specific roles and behaviors designed to influence policy. The need to heed their recommendations is imperative now, given the complex challenges facing higher education. Volkwein (1999) recommends that institutional researchers assume the role of policy analysts who educate the management team in studies on academic affairs, budgeting, student services, and comparative cost studies. Lohmann (1998) advocates that institutional researchers become competent in policy debates and shift studies from mere reporting to timely research on pressing issues in order to become major players in policy development. Bagshaw (1999) convincingly argues that institutional researchers must take the initiative and be skillful teachers in order to have an impact on policy. "Because of their values and knowledge structure, colleges and universities are frequently indisposed to make strategic choices based on institutional research. . . . Consequently, institutional researchers who wish to be successful practitioners by influencing an institution's direction through their research must be skillful teachers as well" (p. 73).

Delaney (1997) recommends that institutional researchers adopt the following strategies to enhance their impact on policy: develop creative ways to shift the focus from mere reporting to research; enhance the capacity for conducting complex studies; create and support high-level audiences for research studies; and expand the focus of research studies to include relevant factors and trends in the external environment.

Emphasizing the importance of incorporating the influence of the external environment in institutional research, Terenzini (1995) observed that while an understanding of the internal culture and politics is essential, the significance of the external context and climate for higher education has increased, and institutional researchers need to identify the demographic, financial, political, and technological developments in the external environment that will be important to the college's future. This is even more crucial now given the current economic climate and global financial challenges.

Results from empirical research also offer ideas to increase institutional researchers' influence on policy. One study investigated institutional researchers' perceptions of effectiveness in influencing policy changes at their institution and identified the following significant behavioral predictors of perceived effectiveness: leaders use the work of institutional research in executive decision making, research reports include policy recommendations, and campuses conduct follow-up studies on the impact of research results. Findings from this study also revealed a significant relationship between policy effectiveness and researchers' professional lives. Those who seek other professionals for advice and are part of a strong professional network perceive that their work achieves greater policy changes at their institution (Delaney, 2001).

In summary, institutional research leaders' recommendations and results from empirical research suggest that institutional researchers need to assume new roles and adopt specific behaviors in order to influence policy. They may need to be teachers and debaters, as well as analysts, who take an active role in translating the results of institutional research findings into recommendations for action.

Increased Involvement in Strategic Planning. Institutional researchers also need to increase their involvement in strategic planning. Through strategic planning, higher education institutions can respond to the demand for accountability and produce evidence that demonstrates effectiveness. Institutional researchers need to be aware of the goals and issues addressed in the strategic planning process so that they can undertake the appropriate studies and produce the required data.

As Voorhees (2008, p. 77) observes, "A strategic plan that focuses on data and uses these data to pose realistic goals and strategies to meet goals portends a significant return for the institution creating it." The institutional research office has a unique opportunity to provide the relevant data for strategic planning if institutional researchers are actively engaged in relevant projects, including student outcome research on retention, transfer, learning outcomes, graduation, and employment rates; admission and program competitor analyses; and correlation studies on curricula with student and employer demands. Furthermore, to fully support the strategic planning process, institutional researchers may need to acquire or strengthen their skills in two key areas: environmental scanning and benchmarking.

Environmental Scanning. Events and trends that occur in the external economic, social, and political environment affect higher education. Environmental scanning provides one method for identifying and understanding these events and trends. This scanning serves as a kind of radar to scan the world systematically to identify trends, developments, and anticipated events. Environmental scanning can identify four types of changes in the external environment: a trend—usually a long-term change in the forces shaping the future of a region or nation; an event—a short-term change in the external event; an emerging issue—a potential controversy arising out of a trend; and a wild card—an event having a low probability of occurrence but a high impact if it does occur (Lapin, 2004).

Benchmarking. Benchmarking involves systematically making comparisons between and among institutions to identify opportunities for improvement and to produce change. A commonly understood type of benchmarking, metric benchmarking, involves the comparison among several institutions of data for selected indicators in order to determine an institution's relative performance (Smith, Armstrong, and Brown, 1999).

According to Swing, good benchmarking enables higher education institutions to identify best practices among similarly situated institutions (Pica, Swing, and Laufgraben, 2004).

Achtemeier and Simpson (2005) offer some advice with regard to applying benchmarking, a tool that grew out of a business culture, in higher education. They note that society has benefited from a view of higher education as a community of scholarship with a culture distinctly different from the corporate culture. Therefore, colleges and universities should not apply benchmarking without an appreciation of those cultural differences. Campuses must balance the business-focused external demands for accountability and efficiency with internal concerns for improvement and effectiveness.

Challenges and Opportunities in Assessment and Accreditation

Increased focus on assessment of student learning, particularly in the accreditation of higher education institutions, offers opportunities and challenges for institutional researchers. The opportunities include offering methodological guidance for the overall assessment process, providing technical and research support in the assessment of student learning, enhancing value to accreditation, and designing new studies to produce assessment results.

Offering Methodological Guidance. Institutional researchers can assume many roles and responsibilities in assessment. They may serve as directors, collaborators, advisors or consultants, and their role may vary during the course of the assessment process. Opportunities to offer methodological guidance occur throughout the assessment process. Methodological issues and tasks to be addressed during the planning stage include identifying and explaining principles of assessment, developing a conceptual model for assessment, identifying institutional policies and practices that promote success, and identifying barriers and strategies to overcome these barriers in assessment (Delaney, 2007).

Methodological knowledge and expertise is particularly crucial to the success of the design phase of assessment. Knowledge of research design, evaluation, measurement, psychometrics, statistics, and analysis should guide critical design considerations. These include determining the overall approach to assessment (formative versus summative), the research design (longitudinal versus cross-sectional), types of measures (direct versus indirect), and desirable characteristics of the measures (validity and reliability).

Institutional researchers can contribute to the success of the implementation phase of assessment by sharing lessons learned from the literature. Previous research provides pertinent insights regarding how to create a positive climate for assessment (Grunwald and Peterson, 2002), promote faculty involvement and satisfaction with assessment (Litterst and Tompkins, 2001), and promote collaboration between academic and student affairs professionals (Banta and Kuh, 1998; Kuh and Banta, 2000).

The analysis and reporting phases of assessment offer occasions for institutional researchers to advise on an overall approach to analysis, identify appropriate statistical techniques, synthesize results from various assessment studies, and offer suggestions regarding reporting assessment results. During the final utilization phase of assessment, the institutional researcher can offer valuable guidance in translating assessment data into information and formulating policy recommendations to promote the use of assessment data.

Providing Technical and Research Support. Bers (2008) identifies specific ways that institutional researchers can provide leadership and assistance in the assessment of student learning. Institutional researchers can help in clearly articulating the knowledge, skills, behaviors, and attitudes that colleges and universities expect students to develop in a course or program. They can identify appropriate approaches to measure whether this learning has occurred and design an assessment plan that identifies responsible individuals and a timetable to ensure that the intended goals are accomplished.

One of the primary resources that institutional researchers bring to assessment is knowledge, access, and expertise in managing data. Institutional researchers can enhance the value of institutional data by linking it to external data sets. With knowledge of measurement principles and techniques, they can also contribute to assessment by designing rubrics and selecting assessment instruments. However, in order for institutional researchers to realize their potential contribution to assessment, they must be present at the assessment table. Institutional researchers need to take the initiative in networking with faculty and those doing assessment to ensure that they are present and involved in the assessment process.

Enhancing Value to Accreditation. Institutional researchers can add significant value to accreditation, provided they are involved in most or all aspects of the accreditation process, including institutional self-assessment, the review teams' visit and written report, the institutional response, and the institution's action plan. Now that regional accreditors are focusing on measurement and use of outcomes to make decisions about institutional effectiveness, it is important for institutional researchers to enhance their understanding of the bigger picture of institutional effectiveness and how the various processes of planning, self-assessment, and improvement can be linked (Dodd, 2004).

Designing New Studies for Assessment. Many typical institutional research studies are potentially relevant for assessment. Examples include senior, alumni, and employer surveys. By focusing on assessment in the design phase, institutional researchers can enhance the relevance of their work to institutional assessment. The research model I employed to design and conduct an assessment-focused senior survey used the following steps:

1. Review the institutional mission.
2. Identify the goals of the undergraduate academic program.
3. Define the major components of the student life experience.

4. Develop a means to evaluate academic achievement and satisfaction.
5. Design an analysis plan to address planning and policy issues.
6. Translate the results into recommendations for planning and policy.

"Expanding Students' Voice in Assessment Through Senior Survey Research" (Delaney, 2005) provides an expanded discussion of the application of this model. It explains how the link between research and policy was achieved by conceptually organizing the study in relation to the institution's mission, the goals of the undergraduate curriculum, and the structure of undergraduate programs; addressing policy relevant questions in the analyses; and developing policy recommendations to capitalize on the college's strengths and enhance areas in need of improvement.

Expanded Role in Program Evaluation. Given the growing emphasis on accountability and effectiveness, campus leaders may call on institutional researchers to engage more fully in formal program evaluation. To serve effectively in this role, institutional researchers should be knowledgeable about evaluation theory and competent in the practice of evaluation.

Deciding whether the purpose of an evaluation is formative or summative and choosing an appropriate evaluation model require knowledge of evaluation theory. *Evaluation Models: Viewpoints on Educational and Human Services Evaluation* (Stufflebeam, Madaus, and Kellaghan, 2000) is an excellent resource that provides the theoretical background and criteria for choosing an evaluation model appropriate to a specific program. Examples of some models include a program objectives–based model in which performance is measured against the objectives; a decision-making model that incorporates the context, input, process, and product components in the evaluation; a model focused on the stakeholders' perspective; and an art criticism model in which the evaluator serves a role similar to that of an art or literary critic. An institutional researcher might design an evaluation based on one model or incorporate ideas from several models.

Institutional researchers should also be competent to manage the implementation phase of an evaluation. The evaluation literature offers several publications to guide this phase. *The Program Evaluation Standards,* sponsored by the Joint Committee on Standards for Educational Evaluation (Sanders, 1994), contains practical guidelines for planning, implementing, and judging evaluations in educational programs. A more recent resource, *A Practical Guide to Program Evaluation Planning* (Holden and Zimmerman, 2008), outlines a step-by-step process to guide evaluators in planning a comprehensive and practical evaluation.

Greater Engagement in Academic Studies. Institutional researchers have traditionally made substantial contributions to administrative programs, including admissions, financial aid, student affairs, and alumni relations. They have been less involved in research on academic programs. This may be due in part to the fact that the institutional research office is associated with the administrative culture rather than the faculty's academic culture, which places a high priority on academic freedom.

Nevertheless, several authors advocate that institutional researchers increase their engagement in their institution's academic life by conducting research on academic issues and providing research support to various constituents. Institutional research might address academic topics such as the intellectual climate of a university, the quality of academic programs, academic standards in courses and programs, and the academic performance of students. Relevant constituencies include accrediting boards, academic councils, educational policy committees, academic deans, chairpersons, and individual faculty members (Delaney, 1997).

Edward St. John (2006) identifies an important role for institutional research in the academic arena. He observes that while higher education research has been theoretically elegant and statistically sophisticated, it has not responded to the new challenge for public accountability. There is a need for strategies for improvement processes within and across disciplines. Institutional research can potentially fulfill this role by setting a minimum standard for inferential research, establishing solid designs for research studies, using both qualitative and quantitative methods, increasing the use of theory, and building collaboration between researchers and practitioners.

Institutional researchers should seek opportunities to collaborate with faculty. They can provide a valuable service to faculty and enhance the scholarly value and intellectual rewards of their own work. In "Why Universities Need Institutional Researchers and Institutional Researchers Need Faculty Members More Than Both Realize," Ehrenberg (2005) discusses how institutional researchers can support faculty by providing access to data. Ehrenberg proposes that institutional researchers and administrators collaborate with faculty in research to inform institutional decision making and the formulation of policy.

Enriching Understanding Through Qualitative Methods. Institutional researchers typically have a strong background in and reliance on quantitative research. However, they also need to develop their competency in qualitative research in order to gain a deeper understanding of the complex issues that decision makers will confront in the future. Van Note Chism and Banta (2007, p. 15) offer a cogent rationale for increased use of qualitative methods: "While there may still be a preference for quantitative expertise in institutional research, we believe long-standing norms are changing as it becomes more apparent that important questions cannot be answered with a single approach. The best decisions are based on a deeper understanding than quantitative methods alone can provide."

Other reasons for increased use of qualitative research include the fact that qualitative methods are generally more accessible, particularly to those who may find statistics daunting. Furthermore, qualitative methods yield findings based in the particular context of the study illuminating the immediate setting and suggesting implications more readily than more abstract methods. Qualitative studies are more holistic in nature and provide insight on several aspects of a setting rather than a narrow focus (Van Note Chism and Banta, 2007). Qualitative data can enhance the meaning and impact of quantitative results. "They enrich a report and help readers understand what is going on. They can enhance our effectiveness as applied researchers by making a situation feel real to the decision-maker we are trying to reach" (Trosset, 2007, p. 21).

Relevant Qualitative Approaches. Researchers may use several qualitative methods to assess academic programs and student services: observation, open-ended interviewing, focus group discussion, and document analysis to complement the data obtained through survey research or quasi-experimental studies (Van Note Chism and Banta, 2007). Focus groups may be particularly helpful in assessing student support services—determining whether potential users even know the services exist and why some aspects of the service may be considered unsatisfactory.

Skills Required for Qualitative Research. Effective use of qualitative research requires many different skills. Trosset (2007) conceptualizes these skills in three dimensions:

• Intellectual skills are necessary to design primary and follow-up questions and to recognize the complexities or implications of what is being said;
• Emotional skills are important for creating the right atmosphere and establishing good rapport; and
• Creativity is critical to perceive unanticipated data or a new idea to pursue during an interview.

Institutional research studies may be most effective when qualitative and quantitative methods are employed in a complementary manner. Both methods are valid forms of inquiry and should be considered along a continuum of methodological approaches. Borland (2001) argues that the most useful research typically results from appropriately applying both methodologies to create knowledge in support of decision making.

New Roles for Institutional Research

In addition to expanding current roles in planning, policy development, and assessment, institutional researchers should consider assuming new roles: serving as postsecondary industry knowledge analysts, developing new programs, and generating new knowledge.

Serving as Postsecondary Industry Knowledge Analysts. Marvin Peterson (1999) predicted that the major challenges confronting higher education would require a shift in the focus of institutional research from organizational improvement to institutional redesign and transformation. He identifies several societal conditions and industry reshaping forces that interact to promote change and consequently require a shift in the focus of institutional research. Examples of influential societal conditions are changing patterns of diversity, the telematics revolution, academic and institutional quality reform, and globalization. Illustrative industry-reshaping forces include innovation in core technology, the threat of new entrants, and substitute services. Higher education leaders need to understand how these conditions and forces affect the higher education environment, and institutional researchers can serve a crucial role in enhancing their understanding.

Peterson (1999) proposes that institutional researchers must become postsecondary knowledge industry analysts and serve as sources of expertise in a new higher education industry paradigm. This new role implies new responsibilities of monitoring social and industry conditions, reviewing strategic options, monitoring the periphery, assessing and reviewing programs, and changing institutional assessment. Institutional researchers need to move beyond the traditional improvement function to becoming management guides. Peterson (1999) contends that "by becoming a proactive management guide to this new industry and environment, institutional research will once again have played its adaptive function—benefiting both the institution and the profession" (p. 103).

Developing New Programs. Voorhees (2005) proposes that institutional researchers play a key role in developing new programs by gathering and analyzing data, raising critical questions, and proposing methods to answer these questions. Relevant questions include: How does the program fit with the institutional role and mission? What is the impact of the program on institutional resources? Is there a pool of prospective students likely to enroll? What is the market for program graduates? In essence, institutional researchers can help their institutions align their programs with the reality of the labor markets.

Generating New Knowledge. Teodorescu (2006) envisions a new role for institutional researchers as creators and managers of knowledge. He contends that as knowledge about higher education institutions becomes more complex, institutional researchers should serve as a critical resource in creating, organizing, and disseminating knowledge throughout the organization. In addition to generating knowledge, institutional researchers should also function as knowledge brokers, linking those who need the knowledge with those who possess it. To function effectively as knowledge managers or knowledge workers, Teodorescu (2006) proposes that institutional researchers will need to possess both hard skills, such as quantitative data analysis and Web development, and soft skills—the ability to form and maintain informal knowledge networks, gather and interpret qualitative data through interviews and direct observation, and the ability to gather stories and triangulate them through qualitative data. Institutional researchers will need to use more narratives and stories in the creation of institutional knowledge.

Requirements for Success

To achieve success in new and expanded roles, institutional researchers and higher education administrators need a shared perspective on the role of institutional research. Administrators' perception of the role of institutional research is crucial: "When institutional research is perceived simply as a number-crunching activity, not only does the profession lose, but so does each and every institution where this attitude prevails" (Presley, 1990, p. 106). Echoing a similar theme, Olsen (2000) observes that while the practice of institutional research involves the production of data, the art is contextualizing the data and converting them into meaningful information.

Administrators' Role. Administrators play a critical role in enabling institutional researchers to produce successful studies. Effective administrators articulate policy-relevant questions, value research, facilitate access to resources, and use the results of research in decision making. Ehrenberg (2005), a former vice president who supervised the office of institutional research at Cornell University, emphasizes the need to educate administrators, particularly if they are not data driven, about the usefulness of institutional research.

Researcher Qualifications. Several studies highlight the importance of researcher qualifications to institutional researchers' effectiveness. Volkwein (1999) observes that the role of the institutional researcher as policy analyst requires relatively high levels of education and training, as well as analytical and issues intelligence. Terenzini (1999) notes that acquiring the methodological and analytical skills relevant to institutional research is most likely to be sound and complete when received in formal course work in such areas as research design, measurement, sampling, statistics, and qualitative research methods. Delaney (2001) found that institutional researchers with a doctorate reported significantly more often that their work had resulted in program or policy changes at their institution. The expanded and new roles discussed in this chapter will require highly educated and skilled institutional research professionals.

Implications for Institutional Research Offices. These roles also bear implications for the configuration of institutional research offices. While the size of institutional research offices may vary, it will be important to include individuals who collectively possess most of the required highly diversified skills and talents.

The qualifications of the director of institutional research are crucial in terms of the leadership role he or she plays in the office and in the higher education community. The director should have the required level of methodological knowledge and skill to conduct research and have credibility in the academic community. He or she should also possess strong leadership ability and creativity. Leadership ability is necessary to direct the work of the office and play an effective role in planning and policy. Creativity is required in designing studies, translating data into information, and developing policy recommendations.

Institutional research staff should include at least one individual who has expertise in quantitative research, including survey design, multivariate statistics, and data analysis. Another professional researcher, with advanced knowledge and training, should assume primary responsibility for qualitative research studies. Technology specialists, with a range of skill levels, will be needed to support data collection, data management, and data processing activities for quantitative and qualitative research studies. A data analyst position would require competency in Excel, Access, and a software data analysis package such as SPSS. A technology application specialist with advanced knowledge and skill would potentially develop, implement, and maintain Web-based and other technology application systems to support the institutional research office agenda.

Finally, intellectual ability is of paramount importance for all institutional research professionals in conducting research studies from the design phase to report writing and in their new roles as knowledge industry analysts, knowledge generators, and knowledge brokers.

References

Achtemeier, S. D., and Simpson, R. D. "Practical Considerations When Using Benchmarking for Accountability in Higher Education." *Innovative Higher Education*, 2005, *30*(2), 117–128.

Bagshaw, M. "Teaching Institutional Research to the Learning-Inhibited Institution." In J. F. Volkwein (ed.), *What Is Institutional Research All About? A Critical and Comprehensive Assessment of the Profession*. New Directions for Institutional Research, no. 104. San Francisco: Jossey Bass, 1999.

Banta, T. W., and Kuh, G. D. "A Missing Link in Assessment." *Change*, 1998, *30*(2), 40–46.

Bers, T. H. "The Role of Institutional Assessment in Assessing Student Learning Outcomes." In D. G. Terkla (ed.), *Institutional Research: More Than Just Data*. New Directions for Higher Education, no. 141, San Francisco: Jossey-Bass, 2008.

Borland Jr., K. W. "Qualitative and Quantitative Research: A Complementary Balance." In R. D. Howard and K. W. Borland Jr. (eds.), *Balancing Qualitative and Quantitative Information for Effective Decision Support*. New Directions for Institutional Research, no. 112, San Francisco: Jossey Bass, 2001.

Delaney, A. M. "The Role of Institutional Research in Higher Education: Enabling Researchers to Meet New Challenges." *Research in Higher Education*, 1997, *38*(1), 1–16.

Delaney, A. M. "Institutional Researchers' Perceptions of Effectiveness." *Research in Higher Education*, 2001, *42*(2), 197–210.

Delaney, A. M. "Expanding Students' Voice in Assessment Through Senior Survey Research." Tallahassee, Fla.: Association for Institutional Research, Summer 2005.

Delaney, A. M. "New Challenges and Opportunities for Institutional Researchers in Assessment and Accreditation." *Tertiary Education Management*, 2007, *13*(1), 61–72.

Dodd, A. H. "Accreditation as a Catalyst for Institutional Effectiveness" In M. J. Dooris, J. M. Kelley, and J. F. Trainer (eds.), *Successful Strategic Planning*. New Directions for Institutional Research, no. 123. San Francisco: Jossey Bass, 2004.

Ehrenberg, R. G. "Why Universities Need Institutional Researchers and Institutional Researchers Need Faculty Members More Than Both Realize." *Research in Higher Education,* 2005, *46*(3), 349–363.

Grunwald, H., and Peterson, M. W. "Factors That Promote Faculty Involvement in and Satisfaction with Institutional and Classroom Student Assessment." Paper presented at the annual forum of the Association for Institutional Research, Toronto, June 4, 2002.

Holden, D. J., and Zimmerman, M. A. *A Practical Guide to Program Evaluation Planning.* Thousand Oaks, Calif.: Sage, 2008.

Kuh, G. D., and Banta, T. W. "Faculty-Student Affairs Collaboration on Assessment-Lessons from the Field." *About Campus,* 2000, *4*(6), 4–11.

Lapin, J. D. "Using External Environmental Scanning and Forecasting to Improve Strategic Planning." *Journal of Applied Research in the Community College,* 2004, *11*(2), 105–113.

Litterst, J. K., and Tompkins, P. "Assessment as a Scholarship of Teaching." *Journal of the Association for Communication Administration,* 2001, *30*(1), 1–12.

Lohmann, D. "Positioning Institutional Research as a Major Player in Policy Decisions: Problems to Solve, Actions to Take." Paper presented at the Thirty-Eighth Forum of the Association for Institutional Research, Minneapolis, May 17–20, 1998.

Olsen, D. "Institutional Research." In L. K. Johnsrud and V. J. Rosser (eds.), *The Work and Career Paths of Midlevel Administrators.* New Directions for Higher Education, no. 111. San Francisco: Jossey-Bass, 2000.

Peterson, M. W. "The Role of Institutional Research: From Improvement to Redesign." In J. F. Volkwein (ed.), *What Is Institutional Research All About? A Critical and Comprehensive Assessment of the Profession.* New Directions for Institutional Research, no. 104. San Francisco: Jossey-Bass, 1999.

Pica, J. A., Swing, R. L., and Laufgraben, J. L. "How Benchmarking Can Help Us Improve What We Do." *About Campus,* 2004, *8*(6), 4–11.

Presley, J. B. "Putting the Building Blocks into Place for Effective Institutional Research." In J. B. Presley (ed.), *Organizing Effective Institutional Research Offices.* New Directions for Institutional Research, no. 66. San Francisco: Jossey-Bass, 1990.

Sanders, J. R. *The Program Evaluation Standards.* (2nd ed.) Thousand Oaks, Calif.: Sage, 1994.

Smith, H., Armstrong, J., and Brown, S. *Benchmarking and Threshold Standards in Higher Education.* London: Kogan Page, 1999.

St. John, E. P. "Lessons Learned: Institutional Research as Support for Academic Improvement." In E. P. St. John and M. Wilkerson (eds.), *Reframing Persistence Research to Improve Academic Success.* New Directions for Institutional Research, no. 130. San Francisco: Jossey-Bass, 2006.

Stufflebeam, D. L., Madaus, G. F., and Kellaghan, T. (eds.). *Evaluation Models: Viewpoints on Educational and Human Services Evaluation.* (2nd ed.) Norwell, Mass: Kluwer, 2000.

Teodorescu, D. "Institutional Researchers as Knowledge Managers in Universities: Envisioning New Roles for the IR Profession." *Tertiary Education and Management,* 2006, *12*(1), 75–88.

Terenzini, P. T. "Evolution and Revolution in Institutional Research." *AIR Currents,* 1995, *33*(7), 3–4.

Terenzini, P. T. "On the Nature of Institutional Research and the Knowledge and Skills It Requires." In J. F. Volkwein (ed.), *What Is Institutional Research All About? A Critical and Comprehensive Assessment of the Profession.* New Directions for Institutional Research, no. 104. San Francisco: Jossey-Bass, 1999.

Trosset, C. "Qualitative Research Methods for Institutional Research." In R. D. Howard (ed.), *Using Mixed Methods in Institutional Research.* Tallahassee, Fla.: Association for Institutional Research, 2007.

Van Note Chism, N., and Banta, T. W. "Enhancing Institutional Assessment Efforts Through Qualitative Methods." In S. R. Harper and S. D. Museus (eds.), *Using Qualitative Methods in Institutional Assessment*. New Directions for Institutional Research, no. 136. San Francisco: Jossey-Bass, 2007.

Volkwein, J. F. "The Four Faces of Institutional Research." In J. F. Volkwein (ed.), *What Is Institutional Research All About? A Critical and Comprehensive Assessment of the Profession*. New Directions for Institutional Research, no. 104. San Francisco: Jossey-Bass, 1999.

Voorhees, R. A. "Institutional Research and New Program Development." In R. A. Voorhees and L. Harvey (eds.), *Workforce Development and Higher Education: A Strategic Role for Institutional Research*. New Directions for Institutional Research, no. 128. San Francisco: Jossey-Bass, 2005.

Voorhees, R. A. "Institutional Research's Role in Strategic Planning." In D. G. Terkla (ed.), *Institutional Research: More Than Just Data*. New Directions for Higher Education, no. 141. San Francisco: Jossey-Bass, 2008.

ANNE MARIE DELANEY *is director of institutional research at Babson College in Wellesley, Massachusetts.*

4

Appropriate staffing is critical to effective institutional research, yet most institutional research offices are chronically understaffed. How many and what types of staffing are needed for the ideal institutional research office, and how can it be achieved?

Laying the Foundation: Institutional Research Office Organization, Staffing, and Career Development

Christina Leimer, Dawn Geronimo Terkla

Staffing is a fundamental component of effective institutional research, yet determining and securing adequate resources can be difficult. In addition, as was noted in an AIR Forum presentation on the Achieving the Dream project (Rincones and Champion, 2008), even when colleges allocate money for positions they have difficulty finding institutional research practitioners. With new institutional research offices developing, existing offices expanding, long-time practitioners retiring, and demands on institutional research increasing, staffing issues—securing adequate funding; hiring, training, and retaining staff; and providing career development opportunities—will be acute.

This chapter addresses three questions. First, what are adequate institutional research staffing levels, and how can institutions achieve them? Second, what skills do institutional researchers need to conduct cutting-edge institutional research? Finally, what do colleges and universities need to do to ensure institutional research professionals' job satisfaction and retention? In addition to answering these questions about the characteristics of the ideal institutional research office of the future, we propose our view of its optimal structure and organizational location.

NEW DIRECTIONS FOR INSTITUTIONAL RESEARCH, no. 143, Fall 2009 © Wiley Periodicals, Inc.
Published online in Wiley InterScience (www.interscience.wiley.com) • DOI: 10.1002/ir.304

Relevant Literature

Over the past five decades, scholars and institutional research professionals have offered evidence, both anecdotal and empirical, regarding the nature of the profession. The literature consists of commentary on the skills needed to be an effective institutional researcher, job satisfaction, and effectiveness among members of the institutional research community, as well as typical staffing, structure, and responsibilities of institutional research offices.

Skills Needed to Be Successful in Institutional Research. The work performed by institutional research requires a broad range of skills. Some of these necessitate formal training, some can be learned on the job, and some come about only through long-term on-the-job experience facilitated through organizational and supervisory assistance.

Terenzini (1999) proposed three interdependent types of organizational intelligence that are necessary for effective institutional research. Technical and analytical intelligence is necessary for entry-level work in institutional research. Facility with databases, spreadsheets, word processing, and graphics packages; knowledge of quantitative and qualitative research methods, statistical techniques, assessment, and program evaluation; and factual knowledge of terminology, data definitions, and methodologies are some of the skills that comprise analytical and technical intelligence. Although skills such as institution-specific terminology and definitions may be, and usually are, deepened and expanded on the job, professionals generally acquire the basics through formal education. Thirty-eight percent of institutional research professionals hold a doctorate (Volkwein, 2008a). Fifty-three percent earned a master's degree. Most commonly, these degrees are in social sciences or education or, to a lesser extent, business. A few are in math, science, or humanities.

The second type of intelligence, issues intelligence, involves knowledge of issues the institution must address, such as enrollment management, budgeting, assessment, and strategic planning. In addition, it is helpful to understand how the institution functions, how it makes formal and informal decisions, and how to work effectively with institutional managers who undertake these activities. Such knowledge and abilities are a distinct skill set and are not inherent in analytical or technical skills. Without such organizational knowledge and interpersonal abilities, institutional researchers will find their effectiveness and influence extremely limited. Course work can provide overall knowledge of higher education, organizational processes, planning, budgeting, governance, and politics, but only job experience will develop a practitioner's institution-specific knowledge. Often practitioners gain such understanding through a combination of course work and job experience.

Contextual intelligence, the third type of intelligence Terenzini (1999) described, requires not only knowledge of the higher education environment, but also an understanding of the intricacies of a particular institution's history, politics, and culture and the external forces that affect it. This type of intelligence also includes the formal and informal ways that the institution does business within the organization and with its external constituencies, as well as respect for the multiple disciplines, attitudes, and values of people at all levels of the organization. Contextual intelligence, Terenzini says, reflects "organizational savvy and wisdom. It is the form of intelligence that earns institutional research and researchers legitimacy, trust, and respect" (p. 25). Institutional researchers acquire this intelligence only on the job, usually over several years, and most effectively through active engagement with institutional leaders in all areas of the organization.

We emphasize the importance of social intelligence, which, in Terenzini's formulation, is a component of issues intelligence. Social intelligence is the ability to get along well with others and to be able to understand and navigate complex social situations (Albrecht, 2006). This form of intelligence is a critical attribute for institutional research professionals at all levels. The extent to which this is a learned skill is debatable; however, it appears to be a skill that individuals can hone over time. Institutional research professionals often find themselves in positions in which they have little direct authority and must rely on negotiating and mediating skills. A high degree of social intelligence facilitates developing collaborative relationships that increase the effectiveness of such indirect means of authority. Having a sense of humor, being able to laugh and appreciate the ironies of many situations, is useful as well, particularly in complex, ambiguous work circumstances. Many even consider sense of humor a survival skill.

Job Satisfaction and Effectiveness. Nationally the percentage of institutional researchers who have been in the field five years or less appears to have increased in the past decade from one-third (Lindquist, 1999) to 39 percent (Knight and Leimer, 2009). The portion that has worked in institutional research for eleven or more years appears to have declined from 40 percent (Lindquist, 1999) to 33 percent (Knight and Leimer, 2009). According to a study of community college institutional researchers (Morest and Jenkins, 2007), there appears to be considerable movement of institutional research personnel among colleges. However, we do not know the actual rate of those leaving the field of institutional research. In a 1995 survey of members of the Southern Association for Institutional Research (Harrington and Chen, 1995), 20 percent were searching for a new position. In a 2008 national survey of Association for Institutional Research members (Knight and Leimer, 2009), 22 percent indicated they plan to leave their organization, and 31 percent said they may leave. Approximately 35 percent said they are thinking about leaving the institutional research field.

Because effective institutional research requires versatile, highly skilled people, such percentages represent a considerable loss of investment in recruitment, training, institutional knowledge, and expertise. All of the forms of intelligence Terenzini delineates take a considerable amount of time to acquire. Even the most fundamental form, analytical and technical intelligence, can take years given the need to learn the often idiosyncratic nature of an institution's data and business processes that affect that data and the breadth of analytical and research tasks one may be asked to perform. Consequently, for an institutional research office to achieve maximum value to an institution, colleges and universities must be intentional about hiring, developing, and retaining institutional research professionals.

Overall job satisfaction, as well as satisfaction with specific elements of the work, is inversely related to employee turnover. In interviews with a select group of established institutional research professionals, Johnson (1982) found that job satisfaction was by far their most important priority. Institutional researchers, like most other professionals, want to contribute to their organization and want their organization to recognize them for their value. They want to see that their institution values their work, and they want to influence campus decision making. Under these conditions, institutional research professionals are generally satisfied and feel they are effective (Fenstemacher, 1982; Sanford, 1983; Harrington and Chen, 1995; Johnson, 1982; Delaney, 2001; Knight, 2006). Some suggest that institutional researchers indicate satisfaction with their work if it is autonomous, fun, and challenging (Delaney, 2001; Fenstemacher, 1982). They also enjoy positions that give them the opportunity to influence others, participate in making decisions, work with good people, and have a variety of professional responsibilities (Johnson, 1982).

Sources of dissatisfaction among institutional research practitioners include a short career ladder (Johnson 1982), limited promotional opportunities (Johnson, 1982; Fenstemacher, 1982; Delaney, 2001; Knight and Leimer, 2009), limited options for career development, stressful job demands (Delaney, 2001; Knight and Leimer, 2009), and excessive workload (Delaney, 2001; Knight, 2006; Knight and Leimer, 2009). Institutional factors that negatively affect their work are red tape, paperwork, routine, an immediate supervisor who does not value research and planning, and insufficient time to make deliberative decisions (Johnson, 1982).

Some sources of dissatisfaction differ for managers and analysts. Directors find it difficult to do their work effectively with inadequate staffing (Huntington and Claggett, 1991; Knight, 2006), in both number and, to a lesser extent, expertise. Additional obstacles to their effectiveness are reporting demands, lack of time, lack of access to decision makers, the perceived role of institutional research, access to and quality of information systems, and inadequate staff training (Huntington and Claggett, 1991). For analysts, stress and dissatisfaction can result from job monotony, lack of variety or opportunity to use their intelligence, not receiving credit for their work, inadequate time to do quality work, pressure to lower their standards, and lack of opportunities to be heard (Delaney, 2001).

Role conflict is a potential source of stress and dissatisfaction as well. Volkwein (1999) states that such conflict can arise when professionals trained to conduct research and analyses are instead required to produce accurate counts, descriptive statistics, and external reporting. Knight,

Moore, and Coperthwaite (1999) postulate that institutional research professionals' perceived effectiveness is a function of both individual and organizational characteristics that can result in a mismatch between executives' and practitioners' expectations of the institutional research role. For example, if executives desire extensive institutional research support in planning, assessment, and policy analysis, but institutional research staff time is dominated with reporting and filling immediate requests such that its ability to support high-level decisions is limited, the mismatch can result in institutional research being perceived by executives as ineffective. Under such conditions, institutional research staff too may perceive themselves as ineffective, and, by extension, job satisfaction suffers.

Typical Institutional Research Offices Today. Institutional research office structure, staffing, and responsibilities differ widely across institutions, so much so that it can be precarious to make general statements about it. However, Volkwein's (2008a) categorization offers a framework that describes typical ways colleges organize institutional research offices. He refers to four types of organizational structures: the craft structure, the adhocracy, the professional bureaucracy, and elaborate profusion. The craft structure is the most common. Usually a one- or two-person office, its primary responsibilities are reporting and responding to internal data requests. This type of institutional research office most commonly exists in institutions with fewer than five thousand students.

The adhocracy has a simple, flat organizational structure with two to three staff members who are generalists. Some staff members hold a doctorate, but most have a master's degree and work experience. These offices sometimes conduct applied research, but the location of the institutional research office within an institution's administrative structure shapes the type of work the office does. For example, institutional research offices that report in academic affairs are more likely to conduct studies of faculty salaries, workload, student ratings of instruction, assessment, and program review. In the president's office, support for planning is prevalent. In student affairs, projects are likely to include campus climate, residential life, the first-year experience, retention, diversity and effectiveness, and improvement of student services. In finance, institutional research commonly performs studies that support resource allocation and revenue projections.

The professional bureaucracy structure is larger and more formally organized. Staffing includes at least four professionals, and usually more, with a range of credentials, specialization, and experience in the field. More than one staff member is likely to hold a doctorate and have more than ten years of institutional research experience. Numerous student and graduate assistants and analysts who are new to the field are common. In this arrangement, sophisticated research is conducted within the office rather than with the support of other institutional units.

"Elaborate profusion" is an arrangement in which institutional research activity is performed in multiple units, usually by a solo researcher. While this arrangement is common in some research universities, we argue that this is not the most efficient way to provide institutional research services to an institution. Volkwein (2008a) sees the craft structure, the adhocracy, and the professional bureaucracy as a continuum of maturing of the profession, with the professional bureaucracy being the most effective method of organizing.

The location of institutional research in the organizational structure and hierarchy varies as well. Most commonly, institutional research is situated in academic affairs (nearly half of offices) and, secondarily, in the president's office (approximately 25 percent). Much less frequently, campuses house institutional research in finance or administration, planning and effectiveness, student affairs, development, or computing and information technology. Frequently the institutional research manager reports directly to a provost or vice president for academic affairs. The next most common reporting line is to a president. Less often, institutional research reports to a nonacademic vice president. Approximately 16 percent of institutional research managers report lower in the organizational structure (Volkwein, 2008b). Making the institutional research manager part of the executive team benefits both executives and the institution. The institutional research manager is an objective voice in the midst of an array of interests and perspectives on a problem or issue, and keeping that person in the loop, close to discussions of institutional concerns, allows institutional research to gear its work toward the intricacies of those concerns (Chambers and Gerek, 2007).

The most common responsibilities and tasks of institutional research include enrollment management and external reporting (Volkwein, 2008b). Other than these tasks, which are nearly universal, the specific responsibilities depend on where campuses situate institutional research.

This overview provides a synopsis of literature about institutional research professionals and staffing of institutional research offices. Based on this knowledge and our combined experience in the field, the rest of the chapter proposes how colleges and universities should structure and staff the ideal institutional research office and how to hire and retain effective institutional research personnel.

Staffing the Institutional Research Office of the Future

Staffing an office obviously depends on the nature and number of responsibilities expected, and any department or unit must fit into the organization's existing structure and culture. Much of the variation in institutional research offices is due to differential needs and cultures of institutions. That said, however, we believe the institutional research office that can best serve higher education institutions generally matches the professional bureaucracy structure that Volkwein described (2008a). In this configuration, staffing should be adequate in both number and expertise. The staff should include those with general knowledge to allow for cross-functional support and enough specialized knowledge to examine issues deeply and conduct sophisticated research. Such an arrangement creates an environment that allows coordination of research, sharing of expertise, and methodological diversity resulting in high-quality, timely research and analysis that directly addresses policy decisions, goals, and institutional operations. This valuable input to the decision-making process can facilitate the discovery of potential solutions and place the institution at an advantage in achieving its goals. The number of staff and type of expertise needed depend on the nature of the work a campus expects from the office and the number of clients the office serves. Offices currently structured in accordance with this model employ six to twenty staff (Volkwein, 2008a).

The ideal office needs a manager whose primary responsibilities are leading, coordinating, monitoring changes in the higher education landscape that have a direct impact on the institution, and contributing as an active campus management team member. Leaders should incorporate institutional research managers into the routine flow of information such that issues and context intelligence develop over time, and they can make strategic and well-informed decisions about the best way to bring the resources of their office to bear on institutional issues. Reporting should be to the president or provost—whichever better positions institutional research to work across organizational lines, grants autonomy, provides access to stakeholders, communicates critical information to the manager, and values, respects, and uses the products and services of the office. Depending on the number and experience of the line staff, a supervisor should monitor progress on projects, ensure accuracy, train personnel, facilitate smooth day-to-day operations, and represent the office in the manager's absence.

Institutional research offices need enough staffing to allow for some specialization, as well as coverage, so that work does not stop during vacations, sick days, or when a position is vacant. Ordinarily this requires a minimum of five professionals. Usually an institutional research office needs an analyst, or someone with a similar title, to handle reporting or to "compile facts and figures" (Volkwein, 2008a). This position does not absolutely require research and statistical training, but it does demand detail orientation, experience using databases, and comfort working with numbers. An analyst must be able to conduct decision-support analyses. The office must have at least one person skilled in research design, multivariate analysis, assessment, evaluation and survey research, preferably more due to the complexity of these methods and the growing demand for such services. These skills are critical to institutional research offices today and tomorrow. In fact, one might argue that it is important that many, if not all, of the analysts possess the combined skill set, with one analyst assuming primary responsibility for a particular area.

If the campuses structure offices to accommodate specific clients or customers, rather than organize them around specific functions, staff size may be even larger with an analyst who specializes in finance support, another who specializes in student services support, another in academic support, and another supporting planning, development, assessment, or accreditation. Such a configuration creates a critical mass and fosters integration and coordination of projects and people where appropriate. Consequently, although the office may appear large, it is likely to be more effective than the same number of staff working in isolation in various units across the institution.

Rather than hiring a database developer or administrator within institutional research, information technology (IT) should support and maintain databases needed for institutional research work. However, making this a reality depends on the degree to which an institution's IT unit is capable of supporting databases designed for research rather than operations. If it is not, either an IT professional will need to be hired within IR or an analyst will need to be appropriately trained to handle these functions as part of their workload. In the event that the institutional research office relies on the campus IT office, an analyst will need some knowledge of computing systems, databases, and software applications in order to serve as the liaison with IT.

Clerical assistance is most effective if the person has a broad knowledge of the institution, a strong aptitude for technology, and an eye for design to be able to develop attractive reports and other communications materials. It also is helpful if this person has the ability to handle details, coordinate communications across campus offices, and keep track of paperwork for time, travel, supplies ordering, inventory, and budgeting. Undergraduate and graduate assistants can supplement the work of the institutional research staff and develop job skills that make them a potential source for recruitment. Such a strategy may lower recruitment costs, maximize the investment already made in training, and help maintain continuity of institutional knowledge.

In addition to the valuable high-quality work such an office would produce, the staff size and expertise allows for mentoring of new professionals. Given the difficulty in hiring and length of training time, mentoring helps new institutional research practitioners gain a solid grasp of the field and may contribute to job satisfaction and retention. Such continuity is a critical characteristic for positions that must accumulate extensive organizational knowledge to be effective.

Many, if not most, institutional research offices are chronically understaffed. Presidents recognize this as a barrier to practitioners' effectiveness (Harrington, Christie, and Chen, 1996), and it is a source of job dissatisfaction among institutional research managers (Huntington and Claggett, 1991; Knight and Leimer, 2009). They, like presidents, perceive inadequate staffing as an obstacle to effectiveness (Knight, 2006; Morest and Jenkins, 2007). With increasing pressure for accountability, assessment, evidence of improvement, and data-informed decision making required by accreditors and other external constituencies, institutional research offices cannot continue to shoulder the responsibility without adequate staff.

NEW DIRECTIONS FOR INSTITUTIONAL RESEARCH • DOI: 10.1002/ir

Studies show a positive correlation between the size of an institutional research office and the size of the institution (Delaney, 1997; Muffo, 1999). Presumably a smaller staff than that of larger institutions can handle the institutional research tasks at smaller institutions. However, factors that have little relationship to the size of the institution may determine institutional research workload. Given that accreditation and accountability requirements are increasingly similar for all colleges and universities, the relationship between the size of the institutional research office and the institution may have more to do with the availability and allocation of resources than the absolute need for institutional research services. Unless other departments conduct specific institutional research tasks and campuses restrict internal requests for data to senior administrators rather than being available to all campus constituents, it is quite probable that the workload, types of projects, and institutional support required of an institutional research office are comparable across sectors and institutional type and size. If this is the case, then relying on institution size or type to determine institutional research office size is an inappropriate staffing strategy. Instead, campuses should conduct a workload analysis to ensure adequate staffing levels and skill sets.

An option that would make the best use of staff resources in a small office and optimize the institutional research professional's expertise would be to configure the institutional research office to focus specifically on policy, issue, and goal-oriented research and analysis. The IT office or the specific unit that generates the operational data needed for the report or request could complete external reporting and many ad hoc data requests. Institutional researchers could coordinate requests and advise these units on appropriate data definitions as needed but would not extract, manipulate, and supply the data. Not only would this strategy make the best use of the individual's training and interest, and consequently avoid the type of role conflict that contributes to job dissatisfaction, but the research and analyses produced would benefit institutional decision making.

Hiring Institutional Research Staff

Very few institutional research professionals earned their degrees with the intention of pursuing institutional research. Given that no academic degree specifically provides preparation to enter institutional research, the field is largely unknown outside higher education. Only in the past few years have a few institutions created certificate programs in institutional research. Consequently, most new institutional research professionals enter with some technical skill set gained through formal social science, education, or business training and possibly some job-related experience in business, government, or another unit within the academy. Given this circumstance, recruiting below the management level generally means hiring people just out of graduate school with little or no work experience or finding people whose work history includes some set of applicable skills but limited knowledge of higher education institutions. Likely gaps in preparation and uncertainty regarding necessary job skills and performance expectations complicate hiring decisions. It is essential to determine the skills and knowledge that are critical for each position in the office.

Technical and analytical skills are essential. Ensuring that applicants can demonstrate these skills is the first order of business when hiring. Requiring applicants to demonstrate their skill set should be part of the interview process. Evaluating these skills is more accurate if applicants know in advance what interviewers expect and if they have ample time to demonstrate their abilities and approach to problems like those they would encounter on a regular basis on the job.

Given that there is so much to learn in institutional research and so much of it involves on-the-job learning, versatility and intelligence are important characteristics to look for in job candidates. How flexible are they? How quickly do they acquire information or cues that constituents need more information? Are they naturally curious? Do they have enough initiative and resourcefulness to search for answers without direction from others? Interviewers should assess these characteristics through questions and scenarios. Managers should design real-world scenarios to give a sense of cognitive style, ability to share or draw on personal experiences, ability to synthesize information to reach conclusions, professionalism, maturity, flexibility, and sense of humor.

As is the case with any other hiring decision, matching the person to the position, and to the existing staff and organization where possible, is critical. Because scenario-type interview questions can reveal how candidates think and display their communication and interpersonal skills, they can be useful in determining a likely fit or mismatch. Matching the candidate's skills and expectations to the job is essential in maximizing job satisfaction, productivity, and retention. In part, the interview process provides the applicants with information about the kinds of tasks and skills the job requires and allows them to consider whether the position will suit them.

It is important for both the manager and applicant that the process reflects the actualities of the job. Role conflict can result in stress and dissatisfaction when expectations about using one's training on the job fails to match assigned tasks. While it is very important to be certain the skills the office requires match the candidate's experience and interest, it is critical that the hiring supervisor be clear to all candidates that higher education requirements are changing and the position is ever evolving. It is not uncommon to hear institutional research professionals lament, "I do everything." Given the current environment of increasing accountability demands and declining resources, it is more than likely that analysts will need to expand their skill set, explore new topics, and perform new and different analyses.

If one were able to write the perfect job description for an ideal institutional research manager, perhaps it would read:

WANTED: Patient, proactive, socially intelligent detective, debunker of myths, and problem solving, storytelling, institutional historian who is able to demonstrate proficiency in the three Terenzini intelligences, has strong leadership ability and managerial experience, and has the tenacity to build a network of colleagues in order to minimize isolation and to be ever vigilant of the external environment.[1]

While this may seem a bit fanciful, it is not too far from reality. An individual who is managing an institutional research office must be patient. Building a sophisticated, mature institutional research function and a culture of evidence takes time. Institutional research offices that resemble the Volkwein professional bureaucracy have been years in the making. While the institutional research manager and other institutional research professionals often find themselves reacting to a situation, the truly effective professionals are the ones who can scan the internal and external environment and develop strategies to address issues that will surely arise in the near future. For instance, once every ten years, every U.S. higher education institution prepares a self-study for reaccreditation. Proactive institutional research professionals constantly monitor the accreditation standards to ensure their institution is in compliance, and if it is not, they make senior administrators aware of potential deficiencies.

Strong leadership characteristics are critical. Institutional research managers are constantly coordinating, collaborating, and bringing together others over whom they have no authority in order to achieve a goal. For example, during the past year in the United States institutional research directors have been working with registrars, admissions officers, human resource specialists, and IT staff to ensure that their institutions will be in compliance with new federal race and ethnicity reporting requirements. Another important leadership characteristic that accomplished institutional research professionals must possess is diplomacy. Institutional research professionals often find themselves in advisory and diplomatic roles. For example, some institutional research professionals routinely attend board meetings. It is not inconceivable that an institutional researcher might need to respond to a politically sensitive question posed by a trustee or provide additional information that supplements or clarifies comments made by a dean or provost.

We cannot overemphasize that the successful institutional research manager must possess a high level of social intelligence, a point illustrated by an ASSESS listserv discussion regarding the skills needed to work in assessment. Although it was not a direct response to the skills required to be an effective institutional research manager, the compiled inventory is germane: "sensitivity, open-mindedness, flexibility, listening, enthusiasm, commitment to learning, sense of humor, ability to see another's perspective, ability to build others' self-confidence, creativity, team-building, problem-solving, a thick skin, tolerance for ambiguity, patience, ability to motivate others, ability to teach, ability to build trust, and the ability to use data to tell a compelling story" (Leimer, forthcoming).

Institutional research director job postings rarely use language requiring management skills or supervisory experience. This is perplexing given the fact that the ability to retain and develop staff is critical to a well-functioning institutional research office. An effective institutional research director must be able to hire, train, discipline, and even terminate an employee.

The institutional research manager must effectively navigate the bureaucratic and, in some instances, union processes and requirements, as well as be out in front of audiences. Some may underestimate the value of being present or visible on campus; however, it is becoming more and more important for institutional research professionals to serve on campus committees, make presentations at college and departmental meetings, and volunteer to spearhead campuswide initiatives. By doing so, the institutional research professional is able to demonstrate the value of using information to make informed decisions and to work continuously to build a campus culture of data-driven decision making.

Retaining Institutional Research Professionals

What do the institution and the institutional research manager need to do to retain staff? No one would dispute the fact that hiring staff entails considerable cost and then training time and money. Nor would anyone argue that given the types of activities in which institutional research offices engage, continuity is beneficial. Members of an institutional research staff with institutional memory and established relationships with other offices and divisions can save time and resources. Consequently retaining staff is important. Unfortunately, this often is difficult to accomplish. Therefore, it is beneficial to explore strategies to keep staff actively engaged in the institution, as well as interested in the work of the office. We present a variety of strategies that have the potential of mitigating the negative aspects of institutional research that contribute to job dissatisfaction: job monotony, lack of variety or opportunity to use their intelligence, not receiving credit for their work, inadequate time to do quality work, pressure to lower their standards, and lack of opportunities to be heard (Delaney, 2001).

Institutional research work can be socially isolating, especially for analysts in a small office. Although some employees are content with minimal social interaction on the job, few are satisfied without evidence that their work is useful to someone and that it makes a difference to the organization. Managers should inform their institutional research staff of the ways others use their work. For the institutional research director, recognizing staff contributions may be an act as simple as forwarding a thank-you e-mail received from a customer or sharing a compliment about the analyst or the office received in a passing hallway exchange.

Inviting senior administrators to meet with the institutional research staff and talk about how they use the data and reports produced by the office can be valuable. These discussions provide the staff with an opportunity to interact with members of the senior leadership team. They also create an environment where those in institutional research can ask senior staff questions, and senior administrators can explain why the work institutional research does is important to them and the institution. Periodically evaluating the office and sharing the results with all staff is a good way to let everyone know how their work contributes to the overall effectiveness of the office and the institution as a whole. It is imperative that the institutional research manager acknowledge the work done by staff and give credit to the authors. At a minimum, the analyst's name should be on every project that leaves the office. If a director receives an invitation to present the results of a study, the analyst who has conducted the analysis should participate in the presentation if possible. Supervisors should be sure to recognize staff contributions to the office and the institution in personnel evaluations and promotions should be given when feasible.

Mentoring is one method that helps new professionals deal with the demands of the field (Delaney, 2001). Mentoring is also an effective method of retaining institutional research staff. Having a mentor can serve to help a new staff member feel welcomed and provide continuing staff with guidance and support and signals that they are part of a profession rather than just employed at a job. Mentoring opportunities for staff take a variety of forms. A manager may serve as an analyst mentor, or an analyst may be encouraged to seek a mentor from another institution. In the latter case, it is helpful to note that many regional associations, as well as the national Association for Institutional Research, provide opportunities for individuals to request a mentor.

Most institutional research practitioners have earned graduate degrees or have job-related experience, or both. In all likelihood, they are expecting to do high-level work that uses their training. Therefore, it is important to provide staff with the opportunity to work on a variety of tasks, new challenges and, when possible, some degree of autonomy. Not all the work performed by an institutional research office is exciting. However, it is within the manager's discretion to provide analysts with some latitude and allow them to use their professional judgment and creativity to look at an issue in a new way, create a new presentation format, or explore an alternative, innovative research technique. To take advantage of an individual's expertise, staff might serve on campus committees. For example, a staff member who conducts assessment-related research could serve on or work with a college's faculty outcomes assessment committee or perhaps work with an accreditation self-study working group.

Managers should try to provide staff with realistic deadlines to complete their work. A concern expressed by analysts that can lead to job dissatisfaction is inadequate time to do a project to their standards of quality or thoroughness. Trade-offs often must be made between the time required for a project and its completeness. It is imperative to explain the situation to staff so they understand the complexities in conducting applied research.

Another activity that has the potential of being energizing is to have staff meet with members of another institutional research office. This activity may involve both offices describing their work and sharing best practices or just good ideas. It provides staff with an opportunity to learn about what other offices are doing, share war stories with individuals who will appreciate the details, and gain a better understanding of the similarities and differences that exist among institutions and offices.

Within the first few months, after the manager has had time to observe a new staff member on the job, the manager should establish a professional development plan. Staff members should be encouraged to take advantage of courses offered at the institution, participate in professional development workshops or seminars, attend professional meetings, and be active in professional associations. In the current economic times, with campuses eliminating or dramatically reducing travel funds, perhaps institutional research staffs can meet with other institutional research professionals in their local area.

A variety of factors contributes to job satisfaction among institutional research analysts and managers. Like analysts, institutional research managers want the campus to use and value their research. They want their perceptions of the institutional research role and expectations and those of executives to match. Some factors have been identified that contribute to the dissatisfaction of managers, including inadequate staffing, ever increasing external reporting demands, insufficient time, limited access to decision makers, the perception of institutional research as bean counters, poor-quality information systems or extraction tools, and inadequate resources available to train staff. The ability to ameliorate some of these factors is within the purview of senior institutional leaders; however, others are simply beyond their control.

Having adequate staffing is critical. Without adequate resources, institutional research managers cannot fulfill expectations. If it is not possible to provide the institutional research office with the necessary resources, then the manager has to have a serious conversation with senior leaders about what to eliminate from the institutional research portfolio.

Institutional research managers believe that decision makers should use their data and research to make informed decisions, and managers feel they are effective when this occurs (Knight, 2006). Interaction with decision makers is important to facilitating the use of institutional research products. For institutional research managers who do not have access to senior leaders, colleges and universities should create a place at the decision-making table so that the campuses can use institutional research managers' expertise. Especially in today's climate, the institution will make better decisions if an advisor is able to draw conclusions and make recommendations based on sound research, analyses, and knowledge of higher education and the institution.

Conclusion

We have highlighted the critical elements required to create an ideal institutional research office. We have taken a very broad-brush approach, cognizant of the fact that institutional type and sector may have a significant impact on the actual configuration of the function. Yet to optimize the value of institutional research to the institution and higher education in general, colleges and universities must place institutional research appropriately in the organizational structure and hierarchy. They also must sufficiently staff the office with highly trained professionals whose skill sets match the work the institutional research office conducts. Campuses must give considerable thought and care to recruiting and making good hiring decisions. Once hired, institutional researchers should have work that is challenging and interesting, and campuses should offer professional development opportunities in an effort to retain these practitioners and ensure that institutional research is capable of promoting and supporting evidence-based decisions.

References

Albrecht, K. *Social Intelligence: The New Science of Success.* San Francisco: Jossey-Bass, 2006.

Chambers, S., and Gerek, M. L. "Institutional Research Activities." *Institutional Research Applications,* 2007, *12,* 1–23.

Delaney, A. M. "The Role of Institutional Research in Higher Education: Enabling Researchers to Meet New Challenges." *Research in Higher Education,* 1997, *38*(1), 1–16.

Delaney, A. M. "Institutional Researchers: Challenges, Resources and Opportunities." Paper presented at the Forty-First Annual Association for Institutional Research Forum, Long Beach, Calif., June 3–6, 2001.

Fenstemacher, W. P. "Institutional Research Director: Professional Development and Career Path." Tallahassee, Fla.: Association for Institutional Research, 1982.

Harrington, C., and Chen, H. Y. "The Characteristics, Roles and Functions of Institutional Research Professionals in the Southern Association for Institutional Research." Paper presented at the Thirty-Fifth Annual AIR Forum, Boston, May 28–31, 1995.

Harrington, C. F., Christie, R. L., and Chen, H. Y. "Does Institutional Research Really Contribute to Institutional Effectiveness? Perceptions of Institutional Research Effectiveness as Held by College and University Presidents." Paper presented at the Thirty-Sixth Annual AIR Forum, Albuquerque, N. Mex., May 5–8, 1996.

Huntington, R. B., and Claggett, C. A. *Increasing Institutional Research Effectiveness and Productivity: Findings from a National Survey.* Baltimore: University of Maryland, and Largo, Md.: Prince George's Community College, 1991.

Johnson, M. D. "Career Development in Institutional Research." Tallahassee, Fla.: Association for Institutional Research, 1982.

Knight, W. E. "In Their Own Words: Effectiveness in Institutional Research." Paper presented at the Thirty-Third Annual Northeast Association for Institutional Research Conference, Nov. 4–7, Philadelphia, 2006.

Knight, W., and Leimer, C. "Will Institutional Research Staff Stick? An Exploration of Institutional Researchers' Intentions to Remain In or Leave Their Jobs." Unpublished manuscript, 2009.

Knight, W. E., Moore, M. E., and Coperthwaite, C. A. "Knowledge, Skills, and Effectiveness in Institutional Research." In J. F. Volkwein (ed.), *What Is Institutional Research All About? A Critical and Comprehensive Assessment of the Profession*. New Directions for Institutional Research, no. 104. San Francisco: Jossey-Bass, 1999.

Leimer, C. "The Rise of Institutional Effectiveness: Institutional Research Competitor, Customer, Collaborator or Replacement?" Tallahassee, Fla.: Association for Institutional Research, forthcoming.

Lindquist, S. B. (1999). "A Profile of Institutional Researchers from AIR National Membership Surveys." In J. F. Volkwein (ed.), *What Is Institutional Research All About? A Critical and Comprehensive Assessment of the Profession*. New Directions for Institutional Research, no. 104. San Francisco: Jossey-Bass, 1999.

Morest, V. S., and Jenkins, D. "Institutional Research and the Culture of Evidence at Community Colleges." New York: Community College Research Center, Columbia University, 2007.

Muffo, J. A. "A Comparison of Findings from Regional Studies of Institutional Research Offices." In J. F. Volkwein (ed.), *What Is Institutional Research All About? A Critical and Comprehensive Assessment of the Profession*. New Directions for Institutional Research, no. 104. San Francisco: Jossey-Bass, 1999.

Rincones, R., and Champion, M. P. "Is the Achieving the Dream Initiative Transforming the Role of the Institutional Practitioner?" Paper presented at the Forty-Eighth Annual AIR Forum, Seattle, Wash., May 24–28, 2008.

Sanford, T. R. "Coping Strategies for Job Stress Among Institutional Researchers." Paper presented at the Twenty-Third Annual Meeting of the Association for Institutional Research Forum, Toronto, May 23–26, 1983.

Terenzini, P. T. "On the Nature of Institutional Research and the Knowledge and Skills It Requires." In J. F. Volkwein (ed.), *What Is Institutional Research All About? A Critical and Comprehensive Assessment of the Profession*. New Directions for Institutional Research, no. 104. San Francisco: Jossey-Bass, 1999.

Volkwein, J. F. "The Four Faces of Institutional Research." In J.F. Volkwein (ed.), *What Is Institutional Research All About? A Critical and Comprehensive Assessment of the Profession*. New Directions for Institutional Research, no. 104. San Francisco: Jossey-Bass. 1999.

Volkwein, J. F. "The Foundations and Evolution of Institutional Research." In D. G. Terkla (ed.), *Institutional Research: More Than Just Data*. New Directions for Institutional Research, no. 141. San Francisco: Jossey-Bass, 2008a.

Volkwein, J. F. "National Survey of AIR Members." Preliminary results reported to the Reshaping Institutional Research Listserv by J. Woodell, Sept. 16, 2008b.

Note

1. Kent, A. "Research Director Gets Details So That Others Can See the Big Picture." *University Reporter*, 2008, *13*(2), 5.

CHRISTINA LEIMER *is director of institutional research, assessment, and planning at California State University, Fresno.*

DAWN GERONIMO TERKLA *is associate provost for institutional research, assessment, and evaluation at Tufts University in Medford, Massachusetts.*

5

With increasing demands on institutional research professionals, the need to work more productively and efficiently, as well as to produce higher-quality products and communicate more effectively, is essential. What hardware and software programs can help?

Increasing Demands and Changing Institutional Research Roles: How Technology Can Help

Bao Huynh, Mary Frances Gibbons, Fonda Vera

Despite revolutionary changes in technology, the challenges facing institutional research professionals remain remarkably the same as they were a decade ago. Perusing a volume of *New Directions for Institutional Research* from ten years ago shows institutional research professionals grappling with many of the same issues as we do today. They are still meeting disparate stakeholder demands, developing new skills, adopting new roles, and finding ways to communicate complex information through clear presentation of data (Sanders, 1999). Then as now, they turned to technology for a solution; however, the constant reshuffling of priorities and goals for institutional research professionals and their institutions at large is greater than ever before.

Today institutions must meet external stakeholder requirements in the form of evolving accreditation standards and governmental accountability measures at an accelerating level. These pressures often come with little guidance and even less funding. Company representatives bombard senior leadership, research personnel, faculty, and many other decision makers in higher education with presentations and insist their products "are the answer." Too often the decision makers think of technology as the end itself rather than a means to an end, and they purchase new software and hardware without having clearly defined approaches integrated with the overarching institutional strategic framework. For example, a college professor

was recently overheard lamenting, "If we had [name of software program], then we could be successful." She was speaking to her vice president about some assessment challenges her college was facing. This statement echoes the common notion that a group needs to select technology first and determine their approaches next. But this is backwards. The approach needs to drive decisions about technology; technology should not drive the approach. Hence, if they fail to follow this method, people can end up where they do not need to be and have spent lots of money in getting there.

Technology is the means to the end—the vehicle that supports the process. This approach reinforces the need for data-informed decisions and meaningful collaboration before colleges purchase technology. With this paradigm as the foundation, institutional research professionals can help to develop and maintain the strategic focus of the institution. They can guide senior and departmental leaders in their decisions regarding technology. They can help these leaders decide how technology will help meet their community's educational needs, improve student and employee success, and improve the institution's overall effectiveness.

The question, then, is how the institutional research professional can harness technology for improved data integrity, reporting, research, and communication to enable leadership to make data-informed decisions. The answer to this question can aid institutional research professionals in their quest to support their institutions in meeting some of today's toughest challenges: strategic planning, information analysis, stakeholder support, and data presentation. Technology fails to replace the need for meaningful discussions and viable dialogues about these issues, but in many ways, it can help us work more efficiently and effectively. This chapter focuses on these challenges and the technological support available to help institutional research professionals succeed in meeting them at the institutional and departmental levels.

Strategic Planning: The Framework That Drives Major Technology Decisions

Institutional research professionals generally agree that technology can help them operate more efficiently and effectively. Yet they and other decision makers sometimes fail to recognize the importance of the institution's strategic plan in these decisions. It needs to be the basis for determining the best technology purchases for the institution and for individual departments. Institutional research professionals can help institutions make informed major and minor technology decisions by reminding decision makers that these decisions emanate from the institution's strategic plan. In turn, they can model this behavior in their own departmental purchasing decisions. Often senior leaders must make or approve technology decisions with institution-wide implications, and the need to align those decisions with the strategic plan is obvious. But institutional research can also remind departmental leaders that their technology decisions should support the departmental mission and vision and the institutional framework. The strategic plan provides the framework to guide the institution toward answers to such questions as, *What tool best serves its needs?* What is the return on the institution's investment? Can a more affordable technology work just as well? How will each software program support the existing institutional processes?

Ideally strategic frameworks begin with sharply defined, focused, and easily remembered mission and vision statements that integrate with the institution's well-deployed values (Vera, 2008). Institutional research professionals, through creative use of technologies, can play a critical role in the facilitation, development, and maintenance of the institution's mission, vision, and values. The ultimate success of these foundational items depends on total commitment of senior leadership and input and buy-in from faculty and staff. Feedback gathered through focus groups, appreciative inquiries, and surveys ensures that the strategic framework represents the needs of internal and external stakeholders and fosters an atmosphere of collaboration. Software packages used for qualitative analysis of focus group transcripts, appreciative inquiry results, and survey comments are readily available. Examples of such software include NVivo, TextQuest, WordStat, and QDA-Miner, to name only a few.

Using these technological tools, the researcher can upload documents such as transcripts or even the raw audio or video files for analysis. This can be as simple as counting the frequency of certain key words or phrases or as complex as plotting correspondence analysis. The latter enables the researcher to see graphically the relationships among variables. Many institutional research offices can code and manually sort through open-ended survey comments, especially with small sample sizes. Technology assists research professionals with classifying and sorting through large amounts of text, ensuring that more time is available to spend in identifying key cross-cutting themes. In turn, this enables institutional research professionals to identify stakeholders' needs more accurately and efficiently.

Innovative classroom-response tools like iClicker can increase group participation and inject levity into the serious process of building group consensus. Facilitators can distribute the iClicker, a hand-held device that looks like a remote control, to participants for anonymous, immediate feedback to questions they pose. For example, a facilitator might ask a group of faculty to indicate their level of experience with the department's program review process before embarking on a discussion aimed at reaching consensus regarding which components to include. Facilitators can also use the iClicker to check for understanding or for a quick group vote. The novelty of the device provides fun, and the anonymity of the responses helps to put everyone at ease. Thus, the facilitator gains immediate feedback to steer the discussion or understand the audience's ideas.

NEW DIRECTIONS FOR INSTITUTIONAL RESEARCH • DOI: 10.1002/ir

Affordable and user-friendly online survey packages extend the reach of feedback gathering further into the community served by the institution. After training from the software's provided tutorials, institutional research professionals can get feedback from constituents using e-mail addresses stored in an institution's enterprise resource planning (ERP) system or other databases. Most online survey software programs are equipped to compute simple frequencies and averages, while more sophisticated packages can process multivariate statistics.

A comprehensive, robust institutional-level measurement system linked directly to institutional goals is essential to any strategic planning framework (Vera, 2008). The measurement system tracks whether the institution is achieving its goals and, more important, whether actions to achieve those goals are taking place, providing accountability and discipline. Without a measurement system, all the effort put into creating the strategic framework amounts to little more than an exercise. Institutional research professionals, in collaboration with senior leadership, can use technology to develop and maintain such a measurement system. Electronic dashboards are an effective technological tool for tracking the institution's performance relative to the target of its strategic initiatives. Institutional research professionals can design functional and effective dashboards inexpensively by using Excel spreadsheets. More expensive business intelligence (BI) software options like SAS Business Intelligence System and IBM Cognos offer more robust features. They can provide Web-based query wizards for easier reporting, point-and-click customization of dashboard information, and integrated analysis tools like time series and forecasting. The advantages of the Excel spreadsheet are its lower cost and relative simplicity. Its disadvantage is the initial work required to populate the spreadsheets with data through downloads; however, researchers usually can automate these processes. Advantages of the BI systems include their sophisticated look that appeals to some users and their automated queries. Their disadvantages include high costs and possible data lag due to lack of direct interface with the ERP system.

Creating institution-wide buy-in and understanding of the strategic plan may be an institutional research responsibility. Technology can enhance the institutional research professional's ability to deploy the strategic plan at all levels across the institution. PowerPoint software is an effective tool for communication as part of a presentation or posted on the Web for just-in-time training. Terms, processes, and forms familiar to institutional research professionals can often be foreign to others in the institution, leading to confusion and stalled initiatives. A PowerPoint slide show, posted on the Web before a project or initiative begins, disseminates information to staff quickly and can serve as resource material during the course of the project.

Dedicated e-learning software, including Articulate and Acrobat Connect, leverages the animation of Flash to provide a dynamic avenue for deployment of the strategic plan. Using these programs, institutional research professionals can transform an existing PowerPoint presentation into an interactive Flash presentation, complete with audio. This allows users to view training at their own pace on their desktops. For example, college staff can post presentations with video and audio to the Web for training for new employees and as a refresher for current employees.

Word forms offer a low-cost, user-friendly way to create forms for documenting continuous improvement activities. Often the institutional research professional is involved in coordinating quality enhancement, departmental action plans, process improvement, or even benchmarking. If this information is not documented, institutional research professionals cannot track the activity to completion or analyze it for improvements. Using Word forms, institutional research professionals can create forms in a familiar environment with a minimal learning curve, allowing users to complete expandable fields.

Information Analysis

Over the years, the role and purpose of the institutional research department has evolved to new levels. This has occurred because of the means and methods available to assist them in meeting their challenges in helping the institution achieve its strategic goals. When information was difficult to obtain, having to be gathered, assembled, and shared by hard copy, institutional research professionals were data reporters, providing trend charts and static fact books (Wells, Silk, and Torres, 1999).

With the advent of high-speed networks, client-server systems, and the World Wide Web, the role of institutional research professionals has changed. They have progressed from being data brokers who assemble and report data to knowledge managers who use experience and technical expertise to analyze data for insights they distribute across the institution. Now institutional research professionals are information strategists, integrating their knowledge into the institution's guiding strategic focus for continuous improvement. In this new role, they help senior leaders ask the right questions for making data-informed decisions to execute the strategic plan successfully. Senior leadership may look to institutional research professionals to make sense of the flood of easily acquired data created by common access to increasingly inexpensive technology. Institutional research professionals can make judicious use of technology to distill this mass of data into easily understood, quickly digested morsels to better inform decision making.

Institutional research professionals must continue to ensure the integrity of the data they present, as the a priori trust in the validity of their reports is a cornerstone of the profession. The institutional research office is typically the official source of institutional data. In fulfilling this duty, institutional research professionals become guarantors for data integrity of both the raw data they consume and the interpretative analyses they deliver. One frequent complication is the institutional research professional's lack of control over data input and maintenance used in research and reporting.

To ensure their data access is consistent, accurate, and complete, some institutional research professionals prefer data warehouses that offer static data updated at regular intervals. Before storing data in a warehouse, institutional research professionals can process these data through various data cleaning tools. They check for errors such as misspellings or duplicate records and can populate fields such as missing city and state data based on postal codes. They can also use the data warehouse to compare data for historical trends, providing a useful context of the recent past from which to view present conditions.

To this end, institutional research professionals have many variations of data warehouses from which to choose. The drawback of earlier versions is that the data usually are not operational. To provide the agility necessary to execute the strategic plan successfully, many institutional research professionals advocate maintaining direct access to operational data. In the past decade, colleges have migrated from slow, cumbersome legacy systems to robust ERP systems that seamlessly integrate all functions of the institution into one database. These updated systems can both house historical data and update the data store with new data in real time, effectively creating a real-time data warehouse. Meaningful collaboration between institutional research and frontline staffs like student services counter personnel and division secretaries ensures the quality of the data going into the ERP. This process requires training programs that emphasize correct data entry procedures and explain why the process is important. Improvements in processing power ensure that querying the live database will no longer significantly affect the daily operations of the institution. In turn, institutional research professionals can access these data in real time and provide decision makers with strategic information necessary for identifying just-in-time solutions.

One example of the strategic importance of direct access to operational data is in community colleges (Provasnik and Planty, 2008). Using ERP software for scheduling classes strategically and monitoring seat availability allows institutional research professionals to track classes. It can identify sections that meet capacity and then alert enrollment managers to open more sections before students are lost to competitors. Currently institutional research professionals use uniquery or structured query language (SQL) programming to access live data from ERPs like Datatel's Colleague or Oracle-based systems like People-Soft and SunGard's Banner. They can extend the benefits of programming for live data by working with college senior leadership to demand increased customization of these ERPs. Being able to add file names, field names, or input screens that capture information necessary to the institution's work flow is invaluable. The technology should conform to the institution's requirements rather than change the requirements to match the software's framework.

To take advantage of direct access to live, operational data, institutional research professionals must also have access to robust data manipulation tools. This lets them provide useful analyses and distill knowledge from the vast sea of available data. Often the institutional research office is a top-tier technology user on campus, commanding the latest in hardware powerful enough to handle the various software programs needed to fulfill its different roles. For quantitative analysis, institutional research professionals frequently download large data sets into relatively simple programs like Microsoft Excel and Access or more robust ones like Statistical Analysis Software (SAS) and Statistical Package for Social Sciences (SPSS). More and more of these programs now come with graphic user interface functionality to enable institutional research professionals to deliver information to those who do not have statistical experience. Stakeholders can use desktop readers to display institutional research visualizations and static data in myriad ways, including interactive filtering, sorting, and drill-downs using the Web. An example is Tableau. With this software, analysts can use drag-and-drop functionality to group data, rather than writing complicated code or SQL queries, and display data as multidimensional visualizations that use colors, sizes, and shapes to show magnitude, amount, and trends. With a moderate amount of learning, creating new fields and modifying data displays becomes so quick and efficient that it becomes more important than ever before that institutional research professionals have intimate knowledge of data and the purpose of their projects so that workbooks can be published that are most relevant to the end user rather than publishing everything that the software is capable of producing.

In addition to the quantitative data gleaned from an institution's ERP, technology helps institutional research professionals maintain contact with populations before they become difficult to find to collect primary data. A difficult student population to track down can be an institution's alumni. Alumni associations have worked to engage alumni with the institution and with each other, going beyond simple listservs and blogs. They strive to provide a comprehensive alumni experience in e-networks and online communities that let them share photos and have discussion boards and e-newsletters. They also provide career networking similar to popular social networking sites like Facebook, MySpace, and LinkedIn. In turn, institutional research professionals can tap into these alumni networks to send electronic surveys using the listservs or newsletters.

Geographic information systems (GIS) or computer mapping is a developing field that helps to describe an institution's constituency and searches out underserved populations. It also assists institutional research professionals in executing the institution's strategic plan. GIS allows the visual depiction of data geocoded to a base map. As the demographics of the country change, the ability to answer the question, "What does your constituency look like?" becomes very important. Institutional research professionals can geocode enrollment data against a base map of the college's service area to answer this question. As once expanding communities reach maturity and become built out, institutional research can use GIS to help pinpoint pockets of the community representing underserved markets. In addition, it can identify service area markets where enrollments are particularly strong. For

New Directions for Institutional Research • DOI: 10.1002/ir

example, geocoding the addresses of distance learning students might reveal how far beyond a college's service area its enrollment reaches or how a new rail or other transportation system has affected the enrollment pattern. For institutions that do not draw enrollment primarily from a local service area, geocoding can gauge the efficacy of marketing campaigns targeted for specific regions of the state or nation. It can also assist the sustainability officer with estimating the carbon footprint of commuter students. Continuing to evolve, GIS technology like ArcGIS Server will provide greater Web services. This will allow greater sharing and integrating of geospatial data across all of the institution's departments, with benefits for recruiting, marketing, and economic development.

With the makeup of the institution's constituency identified, other technological advances facilitate the primary data collection. Companies like Scantron have made great advances in hard copy survey scanning software, allowing more sophisticated instruments and quicker, more efficient processing. Not only can users customize questions to fit the task, but they can also control the entire appearance of the survey, from graphics to color, Users can also personalize surveys with names, addresses, or ID codes from a database. The task of administering in-depth survey research becomes less daunting. Institutional research professionals no longer have to weigh the greater response rate traditionally available through hard copy surveys against the labor intensiveness of the data collection.

To meet the digital natives who comprise today's world where they feel most comfortable, some institutional research professionals have taken data collection to new and interesting venues, such as conducting focus groups in alternate reality environments like Second Life (Broitman, 2007). Institutional research professionals hope to translate the greater candor provided by anonymity into insights about student interaction and engagement with online learning and virtual classrooms. Many institutions already have a presence in Second Life, purchasing "islands" on which sit virtual campuses. Institutional research professionals can tap into this existing infrastructure by coordinating with IT or the computer science department to host focus groups.

Support for Key Stakeholders

All of the technologies we have highlighted help institutional research professionals do a better job of research and reporting and supplying the interpretative data college leaders need for making data-informed decisions. Institutional research professionals may also employ this arsenal of technological tools to support key stakeholders in their fulfillment of the institution's strategic plan.

Student success is every college's reason for being. Institutional research professionals can enable the institution to reach its goals in this area by providing support to two key internal stakeholder groups: academic divisions and student services offices. For academic divisions, institutional research offices can use their direct query access to student data and the considerable statistical resources at their disposal. This enables them to assist faculty in crafting actionable, scientifically valid studies of student performance, retention, and persistence. These studies can take the form of electronically administered or in-class surveys or focus groups using facilitation technologies. Institutional research professionals can also play a critical role in the deployment of the strategic plan to the academic divisions. They do this by providing, in collaboration with the chief academic officer, the framework and data for annual program reviews. Institutional research professionals can use technology to query the ERP and supply information using Excel-based reports to instructional deans (segmented by program area). They can provide information about each division's contact hour enrollment, instructional costs, student success measures, faculty diversity, and program market share. In fact, they can provide any metrics necessary for conducting a comprehensive review of each program's health and well-being. The creative use of this technology to support departments' continuous improvement contributes greatly to the institution's overall mission.

For student services, institutional research staff can help track students through their entire educational experience, from predictive analysis of success potential as students enter the institution to graduation and transfer success after students leave the institution. Some institutional leaders have turned to third-party student-tracking software like Estudias by Zogotech to meet the intake demands of disparate departments. Other institutional research professionals find it more cost-effective to advocate for customizing existing ERP to meet this need. For tracking outside the institution, many institutions turn to membership-driven organizations like the National Student Clearinghouse. This enables institutions to upload lists of students using file transfer protocol so they can determine if student cohorts have transferred to other institutions. Such national database systems are cost-effective for student tracking, but voluntary membership hinders the institutional research professional's ability to track students comprehensively. Because many large institutions do not participate in databases like the Clearinghouse, gaps remain in the data returned to researchers. Their efficacy could improve greatly if state governments or the federal government were to mandate participation in this process.

Satisfying accreditation standards and reporting accountability measures to state and federal agencies is a major part of the institutional framework. This challenge requires institutional research professionals to provide services intended for audiences outside the institution and services related to the institution's own intrinsic need to improve. Not only can institutional research professionals supply descriptive data for the institution's accreditation reports, but they can also identify potential opportunities for improvement and performance gaps. With this advantage, the institutional research department can be instrumental in helping the institution identify improvement solutions and work to close the gap. An example of one such issue and use of technology to address the issue is that of faculty credentialing. With increased reliance on adjunct faculty and remote distance education sites, breakdowns in proper documentation of credentials can occur. Access databases populated with course data and cross-listed with faculty credentials can be a powerful tool and a useful check for institutions. This aspect of technology can help them meet this critical standard of accreditation.

Institutional research departments use technology in the role they play in the accrediting agencies' mandated improvement plans. For example, the Southern Association of Colleges and Schools Commission on Colleges require a quality enhancement plan. Liaisons in charge of the plan often are part of or work closely with the institutional research department and use software appropriate for making data-informed decisions. Their goals are to identify and implement plans for improving student learning. In addition, the demand for assessment of student learning outcomes and the push for national accountability have promoted the need for software to help institutional research professionals support faculty and staff in meeting these challenges. To this end, software vendors like Weaveonline, Desire2Learn, Blackboard, and Oracle provide programs to help institutional research professionals, faculty, and staff be successful.

Institutional research professionals can use these technological tools to facilitate the institution's analysis and integration of its mountains of assessment data. Faculty and staff can use them to document and maintain permanent records of activities that assess student learning outcomes and contribute to student success. Using a Web interface, faculty and staff can enter information like work group mission, objectives, measures, and findings into templates, often preset with accreditation requirements. They can use the software's document repository to keep together all assessment information for the cycle. In some software programs, read-and-write privileges can be individually set based on work group roles; in addition, point-and-click report synthesis is available. Although the software may document activity, the real work lies in defining the assessment process and always closing the assessment loop with the clear use of results to realize improvement gains.

Presenting the Data

The field of institutional research requires broad institutional knowledge and highly specialized skills to understand the context of the data and construct analyses effectively that flow logically from those data. To maximize decision makers' use of data and ensure they retain their hard-gained insights, institutional research professionals must consider how they deliver their key products and services. They can use technology to create reports viewed as they intended them to be. They are clear and visually appealing, and users can view them on demand from various venues.

As is true with the integrity in the data they use, institutional research professionals must ensure integrity in the data they present. Portable docu-

NEW DIRECTIONS FOR INSTITUTIONAL RESEARCH • DOI: 10.1002/ir

ment format programs like those from Adobe allow institutional research professionals to present findings as they intended, with no alterations and all caveats.

In addition to building confidence in the information they provide, institutional research professionals deliver reports that are clear, easily understood, and presented attractively. Time spent in discussion with decision makers should be about the implications of the data, not about how to read the report. Today's institutional research professionals must be layout artists, using principles of good page design and judicious color selections. Software to help with this process can be simple and straightforward like Microsoft Office's suite of products, or it can be a more powerful software program with a steeper learning curve, such as Adobe Indesign, Quark Xpress, or Adobe Illustrator. These robust graphics packages offer greater ability to customize charts, diagrams, and page layouts. Institutional research professionals can plot multivariate statistics, eliminate chart elements like grid lines or bounding boxes that convey no information, and use color and text placement strategically. The monetary costs of the software are minimal compared to the functionality they deliver.

Learning to use the software and developing graphical skill sets outside the institutional research realm may require considerable time and effort. However, the benefits of good information design—clarity and effective presentations—are invaluable, as evidenced in *The Visual Display of Quantitative Information* (Tufte, 2001). Ultimately institutional research offices should find affordable software packages that can help them translate large data sets and statistical analysis into attractive reports. They need to offer information in an easily understood format because this improves the odds that campus constituents will use the data effectively.

Most view Web publishing as a basic requirement in today's networked environment. The Web often serves as not only a means to deliver product but also as a repository of historical data easily accessible by everyone on the institution's intranet. Placing data on the Web has progressed from plain text in HTML tables or static PDF documents to pivot tables that offer a semblance of interactivity. Users can summarize flat data in different ways and provide fully interactive database solutions using programs like Tableau or WebFOCUS. This also allows users to examine data from different perspectives, similar to the functionality of pivotal tables but with built-in visualization. This greater level of interactivity makes data more accessible to audiences because they can sort and view data in informative ways. They do not have to return to institutional research to request a different arrangement.

Many researchers suggest that good research engenders as many questions as it answers. Even with the clearest and most concise printed reports or the most interactive Web interface, institutional research professionals still need to present information to a live audience. Technology can help them avoid presentations that are simply an endless series of bar charts and tables. The use of PowerPoint is ubiquitous, but recently institutional research professionals have used Adobe Flash to show data dynamically.

One example is Google's Motion Chart gadget, which explores several indicators like enrollment or retention over time.

Just like distance learning education, these presentations can occur with audience and presenter great distances apart using a Web conferencing software program like GoToWebinar. Presenters can lead robust discussions with colleagues who otherwise would not participate. Participants can remain at their desks and log into the Web conference using their desktops, telephones, or microphones to interact with each other in real time. Web conferencing companies host these programs, and no additional investments in hardware or infrastructure are required of presenters or participants.

Using their college or university's large bandwidth and the World Wide Web, institutional research professionals share information on demand using streaming media and podcasts. Streaming media, both video and audio, allow users to watch a video file hosted on a server without waiting for the file to download. They view the video in a continuous stream as it arrives on their computers without any files to save. A podcast, a term combining "iPod" and "broadcast," is similar to streaming media except users download the file, which then can be copied, edited, or redistributed. Institutional research professionals can produce streaming media and podcasts at their most basic level in their offices with a webcam and microphone. They can record video and audio and edit the material in software like Apple's iMovie or Window's MovieMaker. Also, they can use free capture and editing programs available on the Internet like Odeo, Hipcast, and Gcast, to name a few. However, the resolution of such a basic production is by its nature poor. If they are producing streaming media, users need access to a media server unless they publish reports at a third-party site like YouTube. For better resolution and more control over distribution, users need to work with the institution's Web and IT office for access to high-quality audio and video equipment and studio lighting. In addition, they will probably host the media on the institution's servers.

Institutional Research Offices in the Twenty-First Century

Today institutional research professionals can find a software program or hardware device to assist them in almost every endeavor. The years ahead will produce even more sophisticated tools that will change the way institutional research professionals work and live. The advances in technology will require them to embrace life-long learning and to be more persuasive in their advocacy of data-informed decision making. Institutional research professionals will continue to influence major institutional technology purchases as well as model the behavior they advocate by their own departmental technology purchases. Indeed, institutional research professionals can harness technology to increase production, maintain quality, and achieve greater effectiveness—the by-product of remembering that technology is the vehicle, not the driver. Institutional research professionals need to work from a foundation of meaningful collaborations among work groups and well-thought-out approaches aligned with the institution's strategic focus. When they do, they can broker informed decisions about which technological innovations will best achieve the goals of the institutional research office of the future.

References

Broitman, A. "Focus Groups Get a Second Life." 2007. Retrieved December 12, 2008, from http://www.imediaconnection.com/content/13875.asp.

Provasnik, S., and Planty, M. Community Colleges: Special Supplement to the Condition of Education." 2008. Retrieved December 12, 2008, from http://nces.ed.gov/pubs2008/2008033.pdf.

Sanders, L. (ed.). *How Technology Is Changing Institutional Research*. New Directions for Institutional Research, no. 103. San Francisco: Jossey-Bass, 1999.

Tufte, E. R. *The Visual Display of Quantitative Information*. Cheshire, Conn.: Graphics Press, 2001.

Vera, F. "From Vision to Outcomes: Building a Comprehensive Continuous Improvement System for High Performance." Paper presented at the Annual Forum of the Association for Institutional Research, Seattle, May 27, 2008.

Wells, J., Silk, E., and Torres, D. "Accountability, Technology, and External Access to Information: Implications for Institutional Research." In L. Sanders (ed.), *How Technology Is Changing Institutional Research*. New Directions for Institutional Research, no. 103. San Francisco: Jossey-Bass, 1999.

BAO HUYNH *is director of institutional research at Richland College in Dallas, Texas.*

MARY FRANCES GIBBONS *is quality enhancement plan faculty liaison at Richland College in Dallas, Texas.*

FONDA VERA *is dean of planning and research for institutional effectiveness at Richland College in Dallas, Texas.*

NEW DIRECTIONS FOR INSTITUTIONAL RESEARCH • DOI: 10.1002/ir

6

It is not uncommon to hear institutional researchers, both those new to an institutional research leadership position and veterans, lamenting their absence from the decision-making table. How can institutional research professionals develop strategies that get us to the table?

Raising the Institutional Research Profile: Assessing the Context and Expanding the Use of Organizational Frames

Kelli A. Parmley

Describing institutional research to those not familiar with our profession can be as challenging as subsequently trying to dispel prevailing myths such as the institutional researcher as bean counter. In addition, it is not uncommon for both veteran and novice institutional research leaders to experience the all-too-familiar Friday afternoon phone call from a vice president or task force chair enumerating a list of vague data needs for a report due the next week. After a few questions and what now sounds like an annoyed caller, you agree to produce something and ask yourself, "Why was I not involved earlier?"

That scenario may be a bit overstated, but it is a common lament among institutional researchers that we are often absent from important institutional policymaking or decision-making discussions. Dawn Terkla highlighted this theme in the editor's reprise in the spring 2008 issue of *New Directions for Institutional Research*: "The authors remind us of the importance of institutional researchers being included in the institutional dialogue. Bringing them into the discussion early allows the institution to be proactive, with the potential of yielding great benefits to the institution" (Terkla, 2008, p. 97).

NEW DIRECTIONS FOR INSTITUTIONAL RESEARCH, no. 143, Fall 2009   © Wiley Periodicals, Inc.
Published online in Wiley InterScience (www.interscience.wiley.com) • DOI: 10.1002/ir.306

Our professional publications and conversations continue to mature with respect to improving our technical and analytical capacity and identifying essential institutional research knowledge and skills and recommended structures, functions, and roles for our offices (Knight, 2003; McLaughlin and Howard, 2001; Serban, 2002; Terenzini, 1993; Volkwein, 2008). Developing the data and analysis, organizing the institutional research function, and staffing our offices for the right mix of knowledge and skills is an essential foundation, but how, as institutional researchers, can we improve the sophistication and maturity in our leadership to increase the regularity of being a voice at the policymaking and decision-making table?

Similar to the concept of rapid cognition explored in the book *Blink* (Gladwell, 2005), where the author evaluates the power of the conclusions people reach in a matter of seconds, institutional researchers can extend their dexterity in assessing the decision-making process at a university by developing a more robust array of organizational frames. The application of four organizational frames "deepens your appreciation and understanding of organizations" (Bolman and Deal, 2008, p. 18). By using this approach, institutional researchers may increase the consistency of being at the table by adding depth and breadth to their view of the college or university decision making. Expanding our frames may identify previously missed opportunities or highlight alternative ways of being effective once at the table.

This chapter describes three aspects of the higher education context that complicate the task of finding the table, examines the contrasting features of four organizational frames (Bolman and Deal, 2008), and suggests practical strategies for raising the institutional research profile and securing a consistent seat at the table.

Assessing the College and University Context

Sometimes finding the table where the decisions are made or important discussions take place is no small challenge. There are informal contexts for decision-making opportunities, similar to the corporate anecdote of the golf course deal. However, there are also some general, albeit unique, features of higher education that merit strategic evaluation by institutional researchers. The following is not an exhaustive list of the unique considerations or features of colleges and universities, but is intended as an illustrative look at three aspects of colleges and universities that affect the nature of the decision-making table in higher education.

Shared Governance. Governance in higher education complicates the decision-making terrain with an array of participants, each with a claim to or stake in the process. The governance context consists of the "structures and processes through which institutional participants interact with and influence each other and communicate with the larger environment" (Birnbaum, 1988, p. 4). The challenge for institutional researchers is to decipher the landscape of informal committees, task forces, standing committees, council or board meetings, legislative hearings, or even collective bargaining venues—none of which exists on an organization chart. Thus, the challenge is understanding where and how to access the table.

Finding a seat at the shared governance table may require that we set aside a rational and analytical perspective and adopt a more political view of decision making. Mortimer and Sathre (2007) specifically highlight the political dynamics of decision making that involve boards, administrators, and faculty: "Governing a university surely is not the same as governing the country, but politically savvy behavior is needed in higher education far more than most would like to admit" (p. xii). This view of shared governance is also consistent with Volkwein's "institutional research as spin doctor" role (2008). For example, an institutional researcher may have to abandon an objective and analytical approach to support campus leaders and trustees to present positive evidence of external accountability. However, becoming more politically savvy does not mean abandoning our ethical and professional commitment to sound data and interpretation, but it does mean that we pay special attention to how constituents use and present information to different audiences. Preparing for a board or council meeting is an example. Contributing to a board agenda is a means for elevating the institutional research profile but often has little to do with presenting elaborate and sophisticated data and analysis. Instead institutional researchers can guide campus leaders through complex information by distilling it into a concise and easily understood format that will quickly educate board members. It may offend our sensibilities as professionals to distill several weeks of painstaking data gathering and analysis down to a series of color-coded indicators for a board presentation. However, it can demonstrate the range of skills institutional research can contribute to sometimes delicate shared governance situations and increase the likelihood of future access to the table.

A strategic planning endeavor is another shared governance context where Mortimer and Sathre (2007) highlight the importance of understanding political dynamics: "Politically savvy planners and presidents realize that planning that makes a difference usually involves reaching agreement about difficult issues rooted in competing values" (p. 109). Clearly this is a policy-making and decision-making table where institutional research should be present and active. However, a strategic planning table with the multiple and often conflicting perspectives of students, faculty, administrators, alumni, and board members may mean that our value there has little to do with the breadth and depth of a beautifully bound package of planning data. Instead, we may need to consider contributing in a different way, at least initially, to reach a long-term goal to bring data and information to the process. In other words, we may contribute our organization and analytical skills in ways that do not directly involve data. Volunteering to record and organize the substantive themes of the discussions can be tedious and time-consuming, but it provides an important strategic opportunity. It allows institutional researchers to influence the agenda by organizing the discussion into a structure that can facilitate dialogue, increase buy-in, and build consensus. An intimate understanding of the themes, issues, and points of disagreement can also provide much-needed insight into long-term data and analytical needs.

Organization of Colleges and Universities. The organizational structure of colleges and universities adds another layer of complexity to the shared governance process. Birnbaum's (1988) four organizational models (collegial, bureaucratic, political, and anarchical) provide useful contrasts for considering unique organizational features in higher education and how they may affect our ability to raise the profile of institutional research at different colleges and universities. A key concept in these models is the degree of tight or loose coupling among the environment, the administrative subsystem, and the technical subsystem (Birnbaum, 1988). For example, the decision-making environment at a large public urban university (anarchical model) typically includes the fluid participation of autonomous actors where the coupling between departments or units is very loose (decision making in one may have little or no direct impact on another). The result may be a decision-making process that is more akin to a stream of problems, solutions, and participants rather than one that is more bureaucratic or hierarchical (Birnbaum, 1988).

The benefit of loose coupling to decision makers in these contexts is the opportunity to find creative solutions to environmental pressures, for example, without a negative effect on other areas of the university if the effort fails. However, an institutional researcher in this environment may have to spend an inordinate amount of time addressing issues of coordination and communication related to getting to the table, along with the basic task of making sure important information is readily accessible to decision makers. In contrast, for an institutional research office at a small, private liberal arts college, the coupling between the administrative and academic systems is tighter, with a greater tendency toward making decisions by consensus (Birnbaum, 1988). In this situation, the challenge for institutional research may not be issues of coordination and communication because the table is readily accessed and more clearly defined, and relatively few are involved. However, in this consensus-driven process, the strategy may be heavily focused on processes designed to create buy in.

Levels of Decision Making. Although our desire may be to increase our participation in institution-level decision making, it is especially important that institutional researchers understand the levels of decision making and the differences in them. Furthermore, if we want to be included and effectively participate in institution-level decision-making processes, it is

NEW DIRECTIONS FOR INSTITUTIONAL RESEARCH • DOI: 10.1002/ir

essential to evaluate at what level of decision making the institutional research office as a whole is investing its time and effort and also targeting its work products. Is institutional research as a whole contributing disproportionately to one level or another? Is this a short-term phenomenon or a long-term problem? How does that affect the goal of increasing participation in institution-level decision-making processes?

In their synthesis of the theoretical literature on decision making, Bess and Dee (2008) highlight the importance of understanding whether a decision-making process is strategic, tactical, or operational: "They differ from one another in terms of time frame, organizational locus, information, risk, number of people involved, idea versus thing orientation, nature of constraints, and repertories employed" (Bess and Dee, 2008, pp. 597–598). Institutional research could be involved appropriately in all levels of decision making, depending on a host of factors. However, the questions are how much of the institutional research office's time is spent at each level, and is it consistent with where the office and its leadership would like institutional research to focus its efforts? For example, the implementation of a new student information system on campus may require that institutional research become immersed in helping the campus address basic operational data needs and report writing. However, if institutional research does not build the capacity of functional units on campus to meet its own operational decision-making needs, it becomes profoundly difficult to engage in data collection and analysis that will inform institutional-level decision making.

Getting to the strategic level of discussion and decision making is an essential role for institutional research, given our ability to bring Terenzini's third tier of contextual intelligence (1993) to the table. However, the strategic level of decision making, relative to tactical or operational decision making, has a longer time horizon and a larger number of people involved, tends to be focused on idea creation, is constrained by uncertainty, and has little in the way of a routine approach, and thus a different need for data and information (Bess and Dee, 2008). While we, and our staff, may be more comfortable addressing the operational and tactical needs of campus managers, developing strategies and a skill set for success in the strategic context is unavoidable if the goal is to raise the institutional research profile and contribute at that level.

Bolman and Deal's Four Organizational Frames

Shared governance, the organization of higher education, and differences in decision-making levels are just three illustrations of unique aspects of universities that institutional researchers may want to be part of. However, regardless of organizational arrangements, institutional researchers can benefit from a more robust view of their colleges and universities by using a multiorganizational frame (Bolman and Deal, 2008). Bolman and Deal (2008) describe a frame as a "mental model—a set of ideas and assumptions—that you can carry in your head to help you understand and negotiate a particular territory" (p. 11). Developing a more robust multiframe approach to understanding the decision-making process can provide important insight into improving strategies for raising the institutional research profile as well as contributing more effectively when we are actually at the table.

As institutional researchers continue on the quest to raise the profile of institutional research and intervene sooner in the decision-making discussion, one approach is to expand the use of the multiple organization frames that Bolman and Deal (2008) identified. Framing involves "matching mental maps to circumstances. Reframing requires another skill—the ability to break frames" (Bolman and Deal, 2008, p. 12). By consciously moving beyond a singular approach to understanding colleges and universities and adopting the use of Bolman and Deal's four frames, institutional researchers can potentially shed light on ambiguous and complex situations, adjust their leadership strategies, and demonstrate broad knowledge and skills that can raise the institutional research profile.

The structural frame focuses on organizational design and considers issues from the perspective of the allocation of responsibilities within that structure and how to focus diverse efforts toward a common purpose (Bolman and Deal, 2008). The human resource frame views the organization from the perspective of people as resources that organizations cultivate and retain, giving consideration to, for example, professional development and building organizational commitment (Bolman and Deal, 2008). The political frame ignores formal structure and views organizations as a swirl of coalitions, looks at the distribution of power (distinguishing between formal authority and influence), and accepts conflict as a natural part of organizational life (Bolman and Deal, 2008). Finally, the symbolic frame moves leaders far from rationality and logic and seeks to understand organizational symbols for the meaning and belief that underlies them (Bolman and Deal, 2008). Bolman and Deal specify key assumptions of each frame that provides more detailed insight into the contrasting perspectives of each of these frames.

Structural Leaders. Two important and relevant characteristics of structural leaders are the focus on implementation and experimentation. As structural leaders, institutional researchers with an analytical mindset and knowledge of the organization can bring a much-needed analytical and architectural focus on how campuses implement decisions. However, it is also important for institutional researchers to frame implementation from the perspective of building support where needed (human resource frame) and identifying important coalitions or groups that could exercise influence in the implementation process (political frame). Institutional researchers may not be involved in restructuring efforts for the university, but they can experiment with the structure and function of their own offices to most effectively distribute responsibilities and organize work.

NEW DIRECTIONS FOR INSTITUTIONAL RESEARCH • DOI: 10.1002/ir

Human Resource Frame. Two additional characteristics from this frame are also relevant to institutional research and raising the institutional research profile. Leaders in this frame are "visible and accessible" and "empower others" (Bolman and Deal, 2008, pp. 362–363). Depending on the physical location of institutional research on campus and the history of institutional research's visibility, it may be an important strategy to communicate accessibility by being present at an array of different types of events or meetings and holding meetings at alternative locations. Furthermore, it is important to mentor and empower institutional research staff as partners to do similar outreach and promote the accessibility of institutional research. A substantial part of our task, to truly elevate the profile of institutional research, is to make our terminology and analysis intellectually accessible to those who may find it unfamiliar. How many times are we not invited to the table because we continue to speak a language that key decision makers don't understand?

Political Frame. The political leader is a keen assessor of the distribution of "power and interests" and "builds linkages to key stakeholders" (Bolman and Deal, 2008, p. 365). This is perhaps the frame from which institutional researchers have the most to gain in raising the institutional research profile. I can recall a lesson from a former mentor who, prior to arriving on campus, asked the provost to identify people instrumental in getting things done. He then proceeded to meet with each of these people within the early weeks of arriving on campus. The lesson I took away from that experience was the value in assessing the distribution of power and interests, regardless of formal title or position, and their potential impact on policymaking and decision making on campus. In addition, although the work of institutional research is often technical and tedious, it is essential to use interpersonal skills to build relationships with important constituents. Networking and cultivating relationships, especially with those who can be advocates for getting institutional research to the table, can make a key difference.

Symbolic Frame. Perhaps far afield from our professional experience, leaders in this frame "communicate a vision" and "respect and use history" (Bolman and Deal, 2008, p. 371). Along these lines, being able to talk vividly and passionately about a vision for institutional research and its contribution to the future of the college or university should not be underestimated. The variability and complexity of colleges and universities mean that no single approach to a vision or raising the institutional research profile will work at every institution. However, the perspective of the symbolic frame provides insight into the common values and beliefs on our campus. This may provide an opportunity to highlight data and information that might resonate with particular decision makers by tapping into those shared values and beliefs. A campus leadership that is leery of survey results, but passionate about serving first-generation students may begin to value institutional research's contribution if the initial analysis and findings are focused on first-generation students. Understanding what is commonly valued across campus may also suggest ways to present results or tailor how and when a message is delivered to promote institutional research. Consider using campus marketing and public relations resources to enhance your presentation of the vision and use multiple formal and informal opportunities to talk succinctly about your institutional research vision. By also highlighting the historical context and function of institutional research as a strong foundation for the future, it is possible to demonstrate symbolic respect for institutional research and at the same time raise its profile by talking about the future.

Practical Considerations for Raising the Institutional Research Profile

Bolman and Deal's four frames (2008) provide some important insights into the benefit of using multiple organizational frames. My own experience in a large state agency, then a system office, and three very different institutions in three states broadened the perspective from which I understand and assess my own university context. There are frames in which I am comfortable operating and those that challenge my comfort zone. I can also recognize the frames that colleagues use or do not use as well to potentially fill gaps in perspectives not represented at the table. The following suggestions from my own experience represent a multiframe approach to elevating the profile of institutional research and increasing the likelihood of being at the table.

Assess the Organizational Effectiveness of the Institutional Research Function on Campus. Volkwein's comparison (2008) of the function and customer organization of institutional research is a valuable tool to consider the way in which an institutional research function is structured and organized. Assessing your current institutional research function relative to an ideal form, like the customer organization, can help you understand gaps and strengths. Do "customers" know who to contact for what? Does the organization of your Web site reinforce the structural form? If other aspects of the institutional research function are the responsibility of other units (for example, assessment) on campus, do campus constituents understand this?

Talk About Institutional Research Values and Vision—A Lot. If we find it difficult to describe to those close to us what we do, imagine how difficult it is for those at a distance to understand the structure, function, and role of institutional research. Early in my career, a faculty member asked me about my office. The only association she could make was, "Oh, you administer those awful student evaluations of instruction," and I knew that I needed to do a better job of talking about the breadth and depth of our office. Do not underestimate the value of distilling the values and vision of institutional research to a handful of bullets and, where possible, a graphic display. Find as many informal and formal opportunities as possible to talk about the vision for institutional research. In addition, a simple annual report that identifies progress toward that vision will continue to reinforce and communicate it.

Develop Institutional Research Ambassadors. It is one thing for an institutional research director to talk about the vision and mission for institutional research; it is entirely more powerful when others act as spokespeople. I was stunned when a colleague advocated in a very public forum for institutional research involvement as consultant in an important university endeavor and members of the audience nodded in agreement (although they were signing on for more work). It demonstrated the power of someone else advocating for institutional research's inclusion at the table. In addition, I have found that taking the time to mentor and empower staff to take on important activities, so that I am not the only face of institutional research, is difficult to accomplish, but essential.

Nurture Individual Relationships with Powerful Players. The reality of raising the institutional research profile is that we have to use the power infrastructure at our colleges and universities. For some, that may be relatively easy, depending on where institutional research reports, but even when the formal structure would suggest power—for example, reporting to the president—there are important relationships to cultivate with people of influence elsewhere on campus. This requires looking at your campus with a political frame versus a structural frame. What individuals provide important access to key decision makers? What individuals are at cabinet-level meetings or are members of decision-making groups? Are there faculty leaders, formal or informal, who are instrumental in shared governance activities? Who develops the agenda for board or council meetings?

Learn the Financial Infrastructure and Language. My budgeting and finance roots may bias me, but I have learned that the knowledge and language of finance has served my institutional research career and office well. Relatively few institutional researchers report to finance and administration. However, it is important that all institutional researchers become conversant in the budget process and finance language of their institution or state. Learn the process, including time frames for key events, and seek out clarification about the language of finance professionals. Ideally, the institutional research function on your campus would play a direct role in that process by supplying descriptive and analytical data. If that is not the case, it will be substantially more difficult to get to this table if you do not understand where in the process to potentially intervene or be able to speak what can be a fundamentally different language.

Increase Your Visibility on Campus. Sometimes I feel that institutional researchers should wear T-shirts that say, "Institutional Researchers Are People Too!" but how often do we take the opportunity to attend university or community events to demonstrate that we are not just a bunch of bean counters? There are many opportunities to participate in campus activities, particularly important symbolic events like graduation and convocation. These are not directly related to institutional research, but participating in these events not only sends a subtle message of commitment to the institution, but provides a way to interact informally with faculty, students, and staff and listen for important messages being delivered by key institutional leaders. The latter is particularly important if leaders call on institutional research to provide information for speechwriting or the presentation of information to the press. Listening to the delivery of that information in those visible contexts can provide insight into the style of key campus leaders.

Look for the Right Opportunities to Take Risks. I have directed my considerations thus far at incrementally raising the institutional research profile and subsequently increasing the likelihood of leaders' asking institutional research to be at the table. However, there are also high-profile, risky opportunities that can expedite the visibility and credibility of institutional research and leave a lasting impression on a range of people across the campus. This requires some careful consideration, but there are many opportunities and, given the workload of most campuses, few instances in which offices turn away volunteers. Accreditation and strategic planning are examples of processes where volunteering to participate and lead not only brings the substantive contribution of institutional research, but also provides visibility if the contribution of institutional research is successful. Task forces are another, potentially more focused and time-limited, opportunity to demonstrate the knowledge, skills, and contribution of institutional research to policymaking and decision-making processes. Opportunities like these can help promote the concept of institutional researchers as consultants during decision-making discussions versus merely the producers of data.

Finally, one area that I believe has particular value to institutional research is leadership for knowledge management endeavors on a campus. This is apparent in the addition of technology as a fifth face of institutional research, including knowledge management activities (Serban, 2002): "Institutional researchers have the potential to become the first generation of chief knowledge officers or knowledge managers in higher education or play key roles in institutional knowledge management teams" (p. 105). A growing number of institutional researchers are becoming involved in these projects and, through them, gaining the ability to shape their direction, support institutional research functions, and raise the profile of institutional research.

Do Not Be Afraid to Make Implementation Recommendations. An institutional research office that is visible and actively engaged on campus is one of the few offices that has a view of almost everything on campus. Also, staff members spend a great deal of time with the details of operating practices in order to understand the nature and quality of data. The result is that institutional research can be in a position not only to identify operational issues and problems, but to make suggestions for improvements in processes or recommend steps in implementing a new policy or program. I have watched staff visibly cringe at the idea of making recommendations or suggesting courses of action, but have not had a negative experience when institutional research has offered those suggestions.

You Can Lead Them to Water, But They May Not Drink. There are moments in our preoccupation with getting the data, doing the analysis, developing the report, and distilling the information to an executive summary when we lose sight of the fact that not all leaders are ready for evidence-based decision making, and some simply do not have time to make the translation to what to do. The former situation may be direct evidence that we need to turn to an alternative organizational frame to see if something else is actually going on at the table. At other times, it simply means we invest our time with those who do want to make decisions based on evidence and focus our attention there. In the latter situation, we need to be mindful that our knowledge of the university and higher education in general often provides us with the unique opportunity to suggest courses of action—in other words, to take a risk and make recommendations that the analyses suggest.

Conclusion

Veteran and new institutional research leaders always have opportunities to improve effectiveness at gaining access to or more effectively participating at the table. Expanding our leadership tool kit in this way can happen by reevaluating the unique organizational features of our own universities. What aspects of our organizational arrangements matter most or have the greatest impact on the decision-making process? Increasing our capacity and skill at viewing situations through multiple frames can identify new opportunities or critical gaps. How does a symbolic versus political view of a task force meeting suggest a more effective way for institutional research to participate? Ideally, this new information and perspective offers us a way to take more informed risks in raising the profile of institutional research and increasing the likelihood that we are at the table.

References

Bess, J. L., and Dee, J. R. *Understanding College and University Organization: Theories for Effective Policy and Practice.* Sterling, Va.: Stylus Publishing, 2008.

Birnbaum, R. *How Colleges Work: The Cybernetics of Academic Organization and Leadership.* San Francisco: Jossey-Bass, 1988.

Bolman, L. G., and Deal, T. E. *Reframing Organizations: Artistry, Choice, and Leadership.* San Francisco: Jossey-Bass, 2008.

Gladwell, M. *Blink: The Power of Thinking Without Thinking.* New York: Time Warner Book Group, 2005.

Knight, W. E. (ed.). *Primer for Institutional Research.* Tallahassee, Fla.: Association for Institutional Research, 2003.

McLaughlin, G., and Howard, R. "Theory, Practice, and Ethics of Institutional Research." In R. D. Howard (ed.), *Institutional Research: Decision Support in Higher Education.* Tallahassee, Fla.: Association for Institutional Research, 2001.

Mortimer, K. P., and Sathre, C. O. *The Art and Politics of Academic Governance: Relations Among Boards, Presidents, and Faculty.* Westport, Conn.: Praeger, 2007.

Serban, A. M. "Knowledge Management: The Fifth Face of Institutional Research." In A. M. Serban and J. Luan (eds.), *Knowledge Management: Building a Competitive Advantage in Higher Education.* New Directions for Institutional Research, no. 113. San Francisco: Jossey-Bass, 2002.

Terenzini, P. T. "On the Nature of Institutional Research and the Knowledge and Skills It Requires." *Journal of Research in Higher Education,* 1993, *34*(1), 1–10.

Terkla, D. G. "Reprise." In D. G. Terkla (ed.), *Institutional Research: More Than Just Data.* New Directions for Institutional Research, no. 141. San Francisco: Jossey-Bass, 2008.

Volkwein, J. F. "The Foundations and Evolution of Institutional Research". In D. G. Terkla (ed.), *Institutional Research: More Than Just Data.* New Directions for Institutional Research, no. 141. San Francisco: Jossey-Bass, 2008.

KELLI A. PARMLEY is assistant vice provost for the center for institutional effectiveness at Virginia Commonwealth University.

7

*By more widely applying its natural characteristics, insti-
tutional research can help foster a broad organizational
view among campus constituents, connect people and
ideas, facilitate collaboration, and stimulate organizational learning that leads to cultural transformation.*

Taking a Broader View: Using Institutional Research's Natural Qualities for Transformation

Christina Leimer

External pressures on higher education are pushing it toward systemic
changes that increasingly necessitate collaboration. Federal grants that call
for interdisciplinary research, public-private partnerships, assessment,
accreditation expectations for a culture of evidence and continuous
improvement, and budget deficits all require individuals and organizations
to collaborate, yet traditional higher education structures do not foster this
style of working (Alfred and Rosevear, 2000; Kezar, 2005; Duke, 2002; Keeling, Underhile, and Wall, 2007). Many describe the organization of colleges
and universities as loosely connected vertical structures. Discipline-based
academic departments, bureaucratic and hierarchical administrative units,
segmented business operations, functional divisions such as academic affairs
and student affairs, foundations, athletics programs, and unions operate in
parallel with one another, all pursuing their own goals with varying degrees
of awareness or support of larger organizational goals and issues. This
vertical structuring results in loosely connected silos that inhibit cross-
disciplinary and cross-functional collaboration, narrow people's view of
their role and its potential impact on the larger organization, and breed
allegiance to their smaller organizational units over the institution as a
whole. Without horizontal processes that bring people and functions
together, institution-wide changes are extremely difficult to accomplish.

Some might consider institutional research, which is a part of the traditional higher education structure, as a silo as well. For example, although our work is institutional in focus, the primary tasks frequently conform to the nature of the unit in which institutional research is located. For example, offices may manage and implement student ratings of instruction and faculty workload if housed in academic affairs and may conduct revenue projections and cost estimates if in finance (Volkwein, 2008). They also may create enrollment projections and conduct surveys of student life if in student affairs. We may not be at the decision-making table because our position is lower in the hierarchical structure than that of decision makers or because colleges and universities house us in a different unit. Campuses may infrequently use our skills in assessing outcomes because we are not faculty, though this effect can be mitigated to some extent if we report in academic affairs (Bers, 2008). In numerous ways, organizational structure limits the degree to which we can apply our skills on behalf of our institutions.

To counter this tendency toward segmentation, college campuses need horizontal processes that bring people and functions together. Institutional research practice contains within it seeds of transformation that can help create such horizontal processes. For example, institutional research professionals are strongly collaborative, sharing methods and assisting colleagues outside our home institutions whenever asked (Bers, 2008). In our own colleges and universities as well, by virtue of how we get our work done, institutional research professionals are used to collaborating and finding ways around systemic obstacles. For instance, without developing relationships with information technology and student services offices, particularly admissions and registration, institutional research work would be impossible. Usually institutional research is not in the same division as these departments. Consequently, successful institutional research practitioners have developed horizontal processes that bridge the divide. Another example is institutional research's natural tendency toward a cross-boundary perspective that develops through our familiarity with most aspects of the institution. Such broad knowledge enables institutional research to take a systems view of the organization (Matier, Sidle, and Hurst, 1994), consider multiple implications of data and research, and disseminate these analyses across departmental, functional, and hierarchical boundaries. A further advantage is that we are usually trusted and seen as an objective party. Consequently we can bring a neutral perspective to contentious issues and allay defensiveness (Bers, 2008). By realizing the broader utility of these natural institutional research characteristics and intentionally applying them to institutional goals, executives and institutional research professionals can use these qualities and skills to help create a more collaborative environment across the institution.

In this chapter, I contend that institutional research can contribute to institutional goals, even transformation, by helping to foster a broader organizational view, operating as a connector and facilitator of collaboration, and stimulating organizational learning.

NEW DIRECTIONS FOR INSTITUTIONAL RESEARCH • DOI: 10.1002/ir

Fostering a Broad Organizational View

The foundation for any intentional large-scale change is a common vision or a shared understanding of issues, problems, or directions. Such a shared view is difficult to create in an organization with many silos. Information does not always filter through the organization. When it does, it may not reach people in a way that they can connect to their own departmental efforts. The result is that they see broad institutional goals as irrelevant to their daily work (Keeling, Underhile, and Wall, 2007).

If institutional research is central to institutional life, instead of on the sidelines or buried within the organization such that it has no influence, visibility, or access to decision makers' discussions, it develops this broad organizational view and can bring together data and studies that help cultivate this perspective in others (Matier, Sidle, and Hurst, 1994; Duke, 2002; Billups and DeLucia, 1990). To develop such shared knowledge, institutional research professionals need to be skilled communicators who keep their multiple audiences in mind. Higher education, like the rest of the world, includes people with varying degrees of familiarity with data and predilections for using it. The style of written and oral reports should match the primary characteristics of the audience and the amount of time and attention they can give to the issue. Placing findings in contexts that are relevant to a particular audience ensures interest. Disseminating findings in multiple forms reaches more people and expands the potential for greater impact. Utilizing these approaches, institutional research can help create a shared knowledge-base from which issues, problems, and directives can be approached.

For example, establishing university-level learning outcomes can be a time-consuming, frustrating experience, especially in a large college or university. Realizing this had been a long-term institutional goal that was getting little traction, my office analyzed National Survey of Student Engagement and Faculty Survey of Student Engagement data to see what students said they learned and what faculty said was most important to them that students learn. The findings identified agreement on several outcomes. Consequently, we posted this research on our Web site and announced its availability to the university community by e-mail, and I sent hard copies of the report with a memo to the provost and faculty committee chairs suggesting that these data be used to help gain consensus.

Prompting Connections and Collaboration

In the process of bringing people together around research on an institutional issue, institutional research can serve as a connector, or prompter of collaborations. One of the detrimental effects of silos and the narrow view and limited interactions they create is the lack of awareness that others are dealing with and trying to resolve some of the same problems. Consequently, individuals repeatedly reinvent the wheel, expending energy they could put to other uses. Institutional research can help connect people who might otherwise be unaware of their common interests or interdependence. In my institutional research role, I have connected people who were working independently to develop alternative revenue streams, helping them to unite their efforts into a single, focused institutional proposal rather than competing requests for start-up funds. I have referred faculty who were assessing particular learning outcomes to others who were measuring those same outcomes.

Institutional research professionals who possess facilitation skills and a systems perspective are exceptionally good at this (Matier, Sidle, and Hurst, 1994). In fact, the trust the campus community usually has in institutional research and the perception that it is an objective party can be very useful in this regard. In a previous position, because of this perception of institutional research, I chaired the institution's budget review and strategic planning committees. Some believed a neutral facilitator could best fill these roles. Through these positions, I was able to educate these committees—comprised of faculty, staff, and administrators—about planning, budgeting, and the relationship between those functions and help them develop a broad view of the organization and its goals. In addition, I was able to connect people through subcommittee work or refer them to others in the organization who were involved in or expressed interest in an issue with which the group was grappling.

The most rewarding aspect for me was hearing from people who were retiring from the budget committee that they would never see the organization the same way again. Decisions they assumed were simple or one-dimensional they now knew to be complex. Issues they thought pertinent only to a particular group, they found to be relevant to many. The long-term benefit to the institution was that more people had a deeper understanding of the organization and a willingness to see the big picture and collaborate when institutional need required it.

Stimulating Organizational Learning

In today's climate of accountability and continuous improvement, the goal is not simply dissemination of data, but the use of evidence for organizational learning. Organizational learning involves "continuously thinking, planning, reviewing, and adapting as an organization" (Duke, 2002, p. 6). This complex mix of structure, culture, and myriad individuals with a variety of motives and perspectives is a "quasi-organic system, learning from its experience, reflecting on its learning, and changing its behavior accordingly" (p. 38). In such an environment, broad dissemination of data is critical but in itself will not prompt institutional reflection or action. Organizational learning occurs through people from different backgrounds, disciplines, and locations in the organizational hierarchy sharing information, discussing ideas in relation to organizational goals and values, and collaboratively reflecting on and making sense of what they see (Duke, 2002;

Billups and DeLucia, 1990). These discussion and sense-making sessions focus on data and research, but they will not happen on their own. Leaders and managers must facilitate and support them.

In the process of disseminating information and building a broad organizational view, institutional research can contribute to organizational learning by relating research findings to institutional mission and values. By doing so, not only does new knowledge about the institution become part of a shared view, but reflection and a reexamination of core commitments reinforce individuals' common purpose and can spark energy for a new perspective or direction. Institutional research can help facilitate such organizational learning by participating in or forming horizontally and vertically mixed work groups, serving on campus committees, hosting open forums, or facilitating retreats at which participants present and discuss relevant data, research, and context (Billups and DeLucia, 1990; Matier, Sidle, and Hurst, 1994).

An example of the effectiveness of institutional research in fostering organizational learning is a student retention initiative in which I was involved. One of the institution's strategic goals was to improve student retention. Another was to maintain financial stability. As budget cuts loomed, I determined that the college would benefit from a combined analysis of these two related issues. My methodology not only showed the number of students we were losing and at what point in their academic career, but the financial ramifications of this attrition. In collaboration with the president and vice president for finance, I presented these data in the context of our mission and goals at a collegewide forum. Conveying these findings and drawing connections between these data and our strategic goals and institutional values galvanized faculty and staff. We formed a retention response team to put initiatives in place to reverse our rising attrition rate, and I worked with the implementers to evaluate the effect of their efforts. The result was a nearly 8 percent increase in student retention over four years.

How Best to Use Institutional Research's Natural Qualities

Colleges and universities should give careful consideration to where they position institutional research in the organizational hierarchy to ensure that its placement supports use of these abilities. The location of an institutional research office affects its functions and influence, inhibits or facilitates interaction, and can result in acceptance or rejection of its work (Ridge, 1978; Nichols, 1990; Nichols and Wolff, 1990; Taylor, 1990; Saupe, 1990; Billups and DeLucia, 1990; Lohmann, 1998; Bers, 2008; Volkwein, 2008). For instance, when a department whose focus is cross-institutional reports to the president or provost, not only do others perceive the work of that office as important, it signals the institution's commitment to that activity (Kezar, 2005). Furthermore, institutional research needs to be placed where it is part of the communications flow and can develop broad operational knowledge and relationships with student and faculty organizations and administrators at all levels (Taylor, 1990). For institutional research to use its skills most effectively in the ways I propose, it should report directly to one of these two executives, and those executives must value institutional research and perceive its role in this way.

Institutional research should work closely with other departments that help establish goals and gauge the institution's success: planning, assessment, program review, accreditation, and institutional effectiveness if separate departments exist. Volkwein (2008) notes strong linkages between these processes, as well as budgeting, at most U.S. institutions of higher education. Such linkages do not always involve formal structural arrangements. However, in their study of community colleges, Morest and Jenkins (2007) found that the most sophisticated use of data in decision making was in institutions that combined institutional research, planning, institutional effectiveness, and assessment into a single department. Whether formally or informally linked, their joint work should spring from the institution's strategic plan and relevant programs and initiatives. Such collaboration will benefit the institution as well as the professionals in these areas. Rather than conducting studies in isolation, their work would build on each other's, resulting in greater focus and depth. There would be a wider range of skills and perspectives to draw on. This is especially important for small institutional research offices where collaboration may help extend productivity and increase job satisfaction. In addition, practitioners would have the opportunity to learn from each other, thereby expanding their own knowledge and skill set.

Institutional research professionals should be proactive (Billups and DeLucia, 1990; Leimer, forthcoming b). They should look for new ways to use their existing skills and be willing to develop new skills that add institutional research value to the institution. They should volunteer to serve on institutional committees, propose research-based solutions to institutional problems, and market institutional research. In a 1996 survey (Harrington, Christie, and Chen), 50 percent of presidents said they perceived institutional research as reactive and perceived passivity as a barrier to institutional research effectiveness. Ninety percent preferred institutional research to be proactive. Doing so "demands a more perceptive, creative, responsive and interactive approach to research" (Billups and DeLucia, 1990, p. 94).

Some institutional research professionals might object to such a role as compromising objectivity. Detachment has long been an institutional research value, usually put forth as necessary to ensure objectivity and unbiased research. To be proactive, institutional research professionals must learn to engage with the campus community without sacrificing objectivity. They must understand the needs and realities of decision makers and ask themselves what data will be most helpful and what methods they can use to ensure those data have maximum impact. Then they must follow through and follow up to find out.

Institutional research practitioners should be conscious of the image of institutional research on their campus and how they influence that image. The perception of institutional research's role and capabilities by senior executives and faculty can affect the work it is allowed or invited to do (Bers, 2008; Leimer, forthcoming b). Institutional research professionals are very aware of and concerned about developing and maintaining a reputation for trustworthiness, accuracy, and expertise. These are institutional research cornerstones. But how else is institutional research perceived? Is institutional research visible and known to a wide array of campus constituents? Being visible requires stepping away from the computer; attending campus events, especially those focused on faculty; volunteering for projects and positions not specifically associated with research; and disseminating and presenting research findings to multiple audiences so that the work of the office becomes familiar.

Do others view the institutional research office as approachable and engaged in institutional goals and issues? Setting data and research findings in the context of the institution's planning goals or issues under discussion by institutional committees creates the perception that institutional research is an engaged participant at the heart of the institution, an "institutional leader and active member of the college team rather than an isolated actor" (Slark, 1990, p. 7). The institutional research Web site serves to support and reinforce this image as well. The Web is institutional research's twenty-four-hour representative. Linking to the strategic plan and offices of planning, assessment, program review, and accreditation reflects an engaged, collaborative institutional research department. Is institutional research seen only as a bean counter or too inflexible to understand the differing needs and realities of its multiple customers? Not all projects need to be precise to the second decimal place, and it is not necessary to report all findings. The degree of precision and amount of detail should match the purpose of the data and the user's preferences (Bers, 2008). This is true of formatting decisions as well (Leimer, forthcoming a). Should researchers present the findings in a table, as statistical output, in graphs, or in bulleted or narrative form? Not only do these choices facilitate the use of data, but tailoring the work shows respect and consideration of customers' background or needs.

When it is desirable to modify institutional research's image and, consequently, its role, the institutional research manager must take steps to achieve the intended effect. Executives and senior leaders can help by appointing institutional research to tasks or committees that support the image change, talking about institutional research from a broader perspective, and lending visible support to the manager's actions. Changing an image is not easy. It requires sustained attention and action across years. Yet the more that institutional research professionals show their value and capabilities, the more opportunities they will get to bring their skills to bear on substantive issues and organizational challenges.

Conclusion

Many authors (Kezar, 2005; Duke, 2002; Keeling, Underhile, and Wall, 2007; Matier, Sidle, and Hurst, 1994) propose a new model of higher education organizations or a style of decision making whose central component is collaboration. This key characteristic helps make full use of all of the institution's resources to increase the likelihood that it will adapt and prosper in the changing external climate. A broad organizational view, horizontal connections and interactions between people and departments, and organizational learning are components of a collaborative culture that are natural to institutional research. At colleges and universities where collaborative-based systems and organizational learning are viewed as the path to the future, using these institutional research qualities can help this transformation emerge.

References

Alfred, R., and Rosevear, S. "Organizational Structure, Management and Leadership for the Future." In A. M. Hoffman and R. W. Summers (eds.), *Managing Colleges and Universities: Issues for Leadership.* Westport, Conn.: Bergin and Garvey, 2000.

Bers, T. H. "The Role of Institutional Assessment in Assessing Student Learning Outcomes." In D. G. Terkla (ed.), *Institutional Research: More Than Just Data.* New Directions for Higher Education, no. 141. San Francisco: Jossey-Bass, 2008.

Billups, F. D., and DeLucia, L. A. "Integrating Institutional Research into the Organization." In J. B. Presley (ed.), *Organizing Effective Institutional Research Offices.* New Directions for Institutional Research, no. 66. San Francisco: Jossey-Bass, 1990.

Duke, C. *Managing the learning university.* Philadelphia: Open University Press, 2002.

Harrington, C. F., Christie, R.L., and Chen, H.Y. (1996). "Does Institutional Research Really Contribute to Institutional Effectiveness?: Perceptions of Institutional Research Effectiveness as Held by College and University Presidents." Paper presented at the Thirty-Sixth Annual AIR Forum, Albuquerque, N. Mex., May 5–8.

Keeling, R. P., Underhile, R., and Wall, A. F. (2007). "Horizontal and Vertical Structures: The Dynamics of Organization in Higher Education." *Liberal Education.* 2007, 93(4), 22–31.

Kezar, A. (2005). "Redesigning for Collaboration Within Higher Education Institutions: An Exploration into the Development Process." *Research in Higher Education,* 2005, 46(7), 831–860.

Leimer, C. "First Get Their Attention: Getting Your Results Used." Tallahassee, Fla.: Association for Institutional Research, forthcoming a.

Leimer, C. "The Rise of Institutional Effectiveness: Institutional research competitor, customer, collaborator or replacement?" Tallahassee, Fla.: Association for Institutional Research, forthcoming b.

Lohmann, D. "Positioning Institutional Research as a Major Player in Policy Decisions: Problems to Solve, Actions to Take." Paper presented at the Thirty-Eighth Annual AIR Forum, Minneapolis, May 17–20, 1998.

Matier, M. W., Sidle, C. C., and Hurst, P. J. "How It Ought to Be: Institutional Researcher's Roles as We Approach the Twenty-First Century." Paper presented at the Thirty-Fourth Annual AIR Forum, New Orleans, May 29–June 1, 1994.

Morest, V. S., and Jenkins, D. "Institutional Research and the Culture of Evidence at Community Colleges." New York: Community College Research Center, Columbia University, 2007.

Nichols, J. O. "The Role of Institutional Research in Implementing Institutional Effectiveness or Outcomes Assessment." Tallahassee, Fla.: Association for Institutional Research, 1990.

Nichols, J. O., and Wolff, L. A. "Organizing for Assessment." In J. B. Presley (ed.), *Organizing Effective Institutional Research Offices.* New Directions for Institutional Research, no. 66. San Francisco: Jossey-Bass, 1990.

Ridge, J. W. "Organizing for Institutional Research." Tallahasee, Fla.: Association for Institutional Research, 1978.

Saupe, J. L. "The Functions of Institutional Research (2nd ed.)." 1990. Retrieved March 8, 2009 from http://www.airweb.org/page.asp?page=85.

Slark, J. (1990). "The Traditional Centralized Model of Institutional Research." *New Directions for Community Colleges,* 72, 5–11.

Taylor, A. L. "Options for Location in the Organizational Structure." In J. B. Presley (ed.), *Organizing Effective Institutional Research Offices.* New Directions for Institutional Research, no. 66. San Francisco: Jossey-Bass, 1990.

Volkwein, J. F. "The Foundations and Evolution of Institutional Research." In D. G. Terkla (ed.) *Institutional Research: More Than Just Data.* New Directions for Institutional Research, no. 141. San Francisco: Jossey-Bass, 2008.

CHRISTINA LEIMER is director of institutional research, assessment, and planning at California State University, Fresno.

NEW DIRECTIONS FOR INSTITUTIONAL RESEARCH • DOI: 10.1002/ir

INDEX

Academic studies, greater involvement in, 34–35
Accountability: and higher education, 17; pressures, as external to organization, 18
Accreditation, enhancing value to, 33
Achieving the Dream: Community Colleges Count initiative (Lumina Foundation), 1, 20, 25–26, 43
Achtemeier, S. D., 32
Acrobat Connect, 62–63
Administrators, and institutional researchers, 38
Adobe Flash, 69–70
Adobe Illustrator, 69
Adobe Indesign, 69
Adobe (PDF format), 68–69
Albrecht, K., 45
Alfred, R., 22, 85
Alumni associations, and technology, 65
ArcGIS Server, 66
Armstrong, J., 31
Articulate (e-learning software), 62–63
Assessment, 32–36; academic studies, greater involvement in, 34–35; designing new studies for, 33–34; methodological knowledge and expertise, 32–33; program evaluation, expanded role in, 34; and qualitative research methods, 35–36; technical and research support, providing, 33
Association for Institutional Research (AIR), 1, 6; and mentoring, 55
Awareness campaign, scaling appropriately, 9
Awareness development phase, 8–10

Bagshaw, M., 30
Baldridge, V., 11, 12, 13
Banner (SunGard), 64
Banta, T. W., 32, 35–36
Barefoot, B. O., 14
Benchmarking, 31–32
Bers, T. H., 33, 86, 89, 91
Bess, J. L., 77
Billups, F. D., 87, 89, 90

Birnbaum, R., 76
Blackboard (software), 68
Blink (Gladwell), 74
Bolman, L. G., 74, 77–79, 80
Borland, K. W. Jr., 36
Brock, T., 20–21
Broitman, A., 66
Brown, S., 31
Building awareness, 8–10

Capture and editing programs, 70
Chambers, S., 48
Champion, M. P., 43
Change agents: awareness, development of, 8–10; awareness development phase, 8–10; and constant minor adjustments, 6–7; envisioning institutional researchers as, 7–14; focus development phase, 10–11; incorporate or replacement phase, 13–14; knowledge-building phase, 11–12; resolve to change phase, 12–13
Chen, H. Y., 20, 45, 46, 50, 90
Christie, R. L., 20, 50, 90
Claggett, C. A., 46, 50
Classroom-response tools, 61
Cohen, M. D., 8
Collaboration, 85–86
Colleague (Datatel), 64
Colleges and universities: context, assessing, 74–76; decision-making levels, 76–77; organizational structure, 75–76
Collins, J., 7
Compliance reporting, compilation of data for, 19
Computer mapping, 65–66
Context, college and university, 74–76
Contingency theory, 9
Coperthwaite, C. A., 23, 47
Creativity, and qualitative research, 36
Crosta, P., 17, 21, 26
Culture of evidence: building, 23–26; business intelligence systems, 21; data organization and accessibility, 21; data warehouses, 21; defined, 18–19;

ease of access to institutional data accurately, failure to assess, 21; establishing, 19; expanded role for research, implications of, 20–21; institutional research, establishing structures to support, 25–26; institutional research staff, 22; mixed methods, advantages of using to build, 23–24; new program development, making research an essential element of, 24–25; obstacles to building, 20–21; and organizational change, 20; organizational structure, 22–23; reliability, 21; shift toward evidence, 19

Data integrity, and institutional research offices, 63–64
Data organization and accessibility, 21
Data presentation, and technology, 68–70
Data sharing consortia, 11
Data warehouses, 21
Deal, T. E., 74, 77–80
Decision flow, 12
Decision making levels, 76–77
Dee, J. R., 77
Delaney, A. M., 2, 22–23, 29, 30, 31, 32, 34, 35, 38, 42, 46, 51, 54, 55
DeLucia, L. A., 87, 89, 90
Desire2Learn (software), 68
Directors of institutional research, 1; call to action, 15; job postings, 54; qualifications of, 38–39
Disciplinary experts, partnering with, 10
Dodd, A. H., 33
Dowd, A. C., 19–20
Duke, C., 85, 87, 88, 92
Dwyer, C. A., 19

E-learning software, 62–63
Ehrenberg, R. G., 35, 38
Electronic dashboards, 62
Emotional skills, and qualitative research, 36
Enterprise resource planning (ERP) system, 62, 65, 67
Environmental scanning, 31
Estudias (Zogotech), 67
Evaluation Models: Viewpoints on Educational and Human Services Evaluation (Stufflebeam/Madaus/Kellaghan), 34
Expanding roles of institutional researchers, 29–42

"Expanding Students' Voice in Assessment Through Senior Survey Research" (Delaney), 34

Fenstemacher, W. P., 46
Fiedler, F. E., 9, 12
Fincher, C., 6
Flywheel metaphor, 7
Focus development phase, 10–11; key tasks, 11
Focus groups, 36
Framing, 78
Framing theory, 10–11

Gcast (software), 70
Geographic information systems (GIS), 65–66
Gerek, M. L., 48
Gibbons, M. F., 2, 59, 71
Gladwell, M., 6, 74
Good to Great (Collins), 7
GoToWebinar (Web conferencing software), 70
Governance in higher education, 74–75
Graphics packages, 69
Grunwald, H., 32

Harrington, C. F, 20, 45, 46, 50, 90
Hipcast (software), 70
Holden, D. J., 34
Howard, R., 74
Human desires to change, 9–10
Human resource frame, 79
Huntington, R. B., 46, 50
Hurst, P. J., 92
Huynh, B., 2, 59, 71

IBM Cognos, 62
iClicker, 61
iMovie, 70
Information analysis, 63–66
Information design, 69
Institution-level decision-making processes, 76–77
Institutional computing capacity, growth in, 5
Institutional-level measurement system, 62
Institutional research: ambassadors, developing, 81; assessing the organizational effectiveness of, 80; broad organizational view, fostering, 87; connections and collaboration, prompting, 87–88; as core administrative function,

17; evolution of skills, 5; financial infrastructure and language, learning, 81; future challenge for, 1; image on campus, 91; implementation recommendations, making, 82–83; incorporating the influence of the external environment in, 30; individual relationships with powerful players, nurturing, 81; natural qualities, using, 89–90; new knowledge generation, 37; new program development, 37; new roles for, 36–37; organizational learning, stimulating, 88–89; primary tasks, 86; relevant literature, 43–48; resistance, dealing with, 83; risk taking, 82; skills needed to be successful in, 44–45; and technology, 2, 59–71; transformation, 85, 93; values and vision, talking about, 80–81; Web site, 91

Institutional research directors, *See* Directors of institutional research

Institutional research managers: leadership characteristics, 53; navigation of bureaucratic/union processes, 54; perfect job description, 52–53; social intelligence, 53–54

Institutional research offices, 45–47; adequate resources, need for, 56; career development, 43; clerical assistance, 50; configuration of, 38; creating opportunities to work in, 26; and data integrity, 63–64; deadlines, 55–56; decision makers, 56–57; enrollment management, 48; external reporting, 48; hiring staff, 51–52; ideal, 49; information technology (IT), 50; job satisfaction/effectiveness, 45–47, 56; mentoring of new professionals, 50; organization, 49–50; professional bureaucracy structure, 48–49; retaining staff, 43, 54–57; senior administrators, inviting to meet staff, 55; staffing, 43, 48–54; technical and analytical skill requirements, 52; and technology, 70–71; typical, 47–48; understaffing, problem of, 50–51; variation in, causes of, 48

Institutional research professional associations, call to action, 15

Institutional research profile, 73–84; raising, 80–83

Institutional researchers: benchmarking, 31–32; capacity development, 14–15; as change agents, 5–16; environmental scanning, 31; expanding roles, 29–42; flywheel metaphor, 7; knowledge, access, and expertise in managing data, 33; models of change management, 6; policy development, enhanced role in, 30–31; and policy making, 73; as postsecondary industry knowledge analysts, 36–37; proactive role of, 90; qualifications, 38; requirements for success, 38–39; role conflict, 52; social isolation for, 54–55; strategic planning, increased involvement in, 31; tipping point theory, 6; versatility and intelligence in, 52; visibility of, increasing, 81–82

Integrated Postsecondary Education Data System, 11, 19

Intellectual skills, and qualitative research, 36

Jenkins, D., 22, 45, 50, 90
Job satisfaction, 45–47, 56
Johnson, M. D., 46
Julius, D. J., 11, 12, 13

Kahneman, D., 10
Keeling, R. P., 92
Kellaghan, T., 34
Kent, A., 53
Kezar, A., 85, 89, 92
Knight, W. E., 23, 45, 46–47, 50, 56, 74
Knowledge-building phase, 11–12
Kotter, J. P., 10
Kuh, G. D., 32

Lapin, J. D., 31
Laufgraben, J. L., 32
Leadership succession plan, 14
Leimer, C., 3, 43, 45, 46, 50, 54, 58, 85, 90, 91, 93
Leinbach, T., 17, 21, 26
Lindquist, S. B., 45
Litterst, J. K., 32
Lohmann, D., 30, 89

Madaus, G. F., 34
March, J. G., 8
Matier, M. W., 92
McLaughlin, G., 74
Mentoring, 50, 55
Methodological knowledge and expertise, 32–33
Meyer, J. W., 19
Microsoft Access, 65

Microsoft Excel, 65, 67
Microsoft Office, 69
Millett, C. M., 19
Moore, M. E., 23, 47
Morest, V. S., 2, 17, 20, 21, 22, 26, 28, 45, 50, 90
Mortimer, K. P., 75
Motion Chart gadget (Google), 70
MovieMaker (Windows), 70
Muffo, J. A., 51

National Evaluation of Achieving the Dream, 20–21
National Student Clearinghouse, 67
Nichols, J. O., 89
Norwalk Community College (NCC): formative evaluation methods, use of, 23–24; indicators applied to subsets of student population, 25; research advisory board, 26; researcher involvement with program development or policy change, 25
NVivo, 61

Odeo (software), 70
Olsen, D., 38
Online survey packages, 62
Oracle (software), 68
Organization of higher education, 75–76, 77
Organizational frames, 77–80; defined, 78; human resource frame, 79; political frame, 79; reframing, 78; structural leaders, 78; symbolic frame, 79–80
Outside forces, influence on change, 9

Parmley, K. A., 2, 73, 84
Payne, D. G., 19
PeopleSoft, 64
Peterson, M., 36–37
Peterson, M. W., 1, 32
Petrides, L., 19
Pfeffer, J., 11, 12, 13
Pica, J. A., 32
Planty, M., 64
Podcasts, 70
Policy development, enhanced role of institutional researchers in, 30–31
Political frame, 79
Portable document format (PDF) programs, 68–69
PowerPoint software, 62–63, 69
Practical Guide to Program Evaluation Planning, A (Holden/Zimmerman), 34

Presley, J. B., 38
Problem definition and evaluation, 5
Professional development plans, development by directors of institutional research units, 15
Program evaluation, expanded role in, 34
Program Evaluation Standards, The (Sanders), 34
Provasnik, S., 64
Public educational institutions, use of data, 19
Purdy. L., 20

QDA-Miner, 61
Qualitative research: relevant approaches, 36; skills required for, 36
Quark Xpress, 69

Reframing, 78
Regional associations, and mentoring, 55
Reid, M., 17, 21, 26
Resolve to change phase, 12–13
Richards, S., 20
Ridge, J. W., 89
Rincones, R., 43
Rodriguez, L., 20
Rogers, E. M., 9
Romero, M., 20
Rosevear, S., 85
Rowan, B., 19
Ruben, B. D., 8

Sanders, J. R., 34
Sanders, L., 59
Sanford, T. R., 46
SAS Business Intelligence System, 62
Sathe, V., 10
Sathre, C. O., 75
Saupe, J. L., 91
Scantron, 66
Schlesinger, P. F., 10
Schools Commission on Colleges, 68
Scott, W. R., 18
Seattle Association for Institutional Research Annual Forum (2008), 1
Second Life, 66
Segmentation, 86
Serban, A. M., 74, 82
Seybert, J., 22
Shared governance, 74–75, 77
Sharing lessons learned from the literature, 32
Shults, C., 22

Sidle, C. C., 92
Silk, E., 63
Simpson, R. D., 32
Slark, J., 91
Smith, H., 31
Soonachan, A., 17, 21, 26
Southern Association of Colleges, 68
St. John, E. P., 35
Statistical Analysis Software (SAS), 65
Statistical Package for Social Sciences (SPSS), 65
Strategic planning, increased involvement, 31
Streaming media, 70
Structural leaders, 78
Structured query language (SQL) programming, 64
Stufflebeam, D. L., 34
Successful college presidents, combination of technical competencies and human skills supporting, 6
Swing, R. L., 2, 5, 11, 16, 32
Symbolic frame, 79–80

Tableau (software), 65, 69
Taylor, A. L., 89, 90
Technology: analysis and integration of assessment data, 68; classroom-response tools, 61; computer mapping, 65–66; data, presentation of, 68–70; e-learning software, 62–63; electronic dashboards, 62; enterprise resource planning (ERP) system, 62, 65, 67; faculty credentialing, 68; framework driving major technology decisions, 60–63; geographic information systems (GIS), 65–66; information analysis, 63–66; Information design, 69; institutional-level measurement system, 62; and institutional research, 2; institutional research, 59–71; institutional research offices, 70–71; key stakeholders, support for, 66–68; and live presentations, 69–70; online survey packages, 62; strategic planning, 60–63; student tracking, 67; Web publishing, 69; Word forms, 63
Teodorescu, D., 37
Terenzini, P. T., 6, 30, 38, 44, 45, 53, 74, 77
Terkla, D. G., 2, 43, 58, 73
TextQuest, 61
Tipping point theory, 6
Tompkins, P., 32
Torres, D., 63
Trosset, C., 36
Tufte, E. R., 69
Tversky, A., 10

Underhile, R., 92
Uniquery programming, 64

Van Note Chism, N., 35–36
Vera, F., 2, 59, 61, 71
Visual Display of Quantitative Information (Tufte), 69
Volkwein, J. F., 30, 38, 44, 46, 47, 48, 49, 53, 74, 75, 80, 86, 89, 90
Voorhees, R. A., 31, 37

Wall, A. F., 92
Weaveonline, 68
Web conferencing software programs, 70
Web publishing, 69
WebFOCUS, 69
Wells, J., 63
"Why Universities Need Institutional Researchers and Institutional Researchers Need Faculty Members More Than Both Realize" (Ehrenberg), 35
Wolff, L. A., 89
Word forms, 63
WordStat, 61

YouTube, 70

Zimmerman, M. A., 34

OTHER TITLES AVAILABLE IN THE
NEW DIRECTIONS FOR INSTITUTIONAL RESEARCH SERIES
Robert K. Toutkoushian, Editor-in-Chief

IR 142   **Conducting Research on Asian Americans in Higher Education**
Samuel D. Museus
This volume of *New Directions for Institutional Research* moves beyond
pervasive oversimplified and preconceived notions about Asian Americans
in higher education and offers new directions in studying this population.
The authors highlight the complexities inherent in the realities of Asian
Americans in higher education. In addition to deconstructing common
misconceptions that lead to the invisibility of Asian Americans in higher
education research, they discuss methodological issues related to disaggre-
gating data, assessing programmatic interventions, conducting campus
climate research, engaging Asian American undergraduates in the research
process, and using critical perspectives related to Asian Americans. They
also discuss key challenges and future directions in research on this
population.
ISBN: 978-04705-29614

IR 141   **Using NSSE in Institutional Research**
Robert M. Gonyea, George D. Kuh
Student engagement is now part of the higher education lexicon in North
America. This *New Directions for Institutional Research* volume explains the
value and relevance of the construct, with an emphasis on how results from
the National Survey of Student Engagement have been used for various
purposes. Because process indicators are often used as proxy measures for
institutional quality, the chapter authors discuss how student engagement
data can help colleges and universities satisfy the demand for more evidence,
accountability, and transparency of student and institutional performance.
The widespread uses of student engagement results have helped to increase
the visibility and importance of campus assessment efforts and of
institutional researchers, who provide campus leaders with objective,
trustworthy data about student and institutional performance.
ISBN: 978-04704-99283

IR 140   **Using Financial and Personnel Data in a Changing World for Institutional
Research**
Nicolas A. Valcik
This volume of *New Directions for Institutional Research* explores the ways in
which financial and human resource data can be used in reporting and
analysis. With public sources of revenue stagnating or declining and tuition
costs increasing, the need for improved efficiencies in an institution's
internal practices has become paramount. An institutional research
department can use financial and human resource data to conduct analyses
of institutional business practices to forecast costs and identify revenue
generation. The chapter authors review the use of personnel, expenditure,
and revenue data in the performance of institutional research from several
perspectives: the role of organizational theory in data mining efforts,
integration of various data sources for effective analyses, methodologies for
more efficient faculty compensation benchmarking, the impact of state
legislative decisions on revenue streams, and return on investment
calculations.
ISBN: 978-04704-68517

IR139   Conducting Institutional Research in Non-Campus-Based Settings
Robert K. Toutkoushian, Tod R. Massa
One aspect of the institutional research (IR) profession that has not been
well documented is the many ways that this research is carried out beyond
the confines of a traditional campus-based IR office. The purpose of this
volume of *New Directions for Institutional Research* is to provide readers with
insight into some of these alternatives and help expand understanding of the
nature of institutional research. The chapters in this volume show how
institutional research is being conducted by public university system offices,
state higher education coordinating boards, institutional-affiliated research
offices, and higher education consultants. Because these entities often do not
have ready access to campus-specific data, they must be creative in finding
ways to obtain data and information that enable them to provide a value-
added function in the field. The chapter authors highlight ways in which
these offices acquire and use information for institutional research.
ISBN: 978-04704-12749

IR138   Legal Applications of Data for Institutional Research
Andrew L. Luna
This volume of *New Directions for Institutional Research* explores the seemingly incongruent forces of statistical reasoning and the law and sheds some
light on how institutional researchers can use the two in a complementary
manner to prevent a legal action or to help support the rebuttal of a prima
facie case (i.e., one that at first glance presents sufficient evidence for the
plaintiff to win the case). Until now, there has been little linkage between
the disciplines of law and statistics. While the legal profession uses statistics
to support an argument, interpretations of statistical outcomes may not
follow scientific reasoning. Similarly, a great piece of statistical theory or a
tried-and-true methodology among institutional research professionals may
be thrown out of court if it fails to meet the rules of evidence or contradicts
current legal standing. The information contained within this volume will
benefit institutional research practitioners and contribute to a more frequent
dialogue concerning the complexities of statistical science within the legal
environment.
ISBN: 978-04703-97619

IR137   Alternative Perspectives in Institutional Planning
Terry T. Ishitani
Institutional planning is coming to the fore in higher education as states,
the federal government, and the public increasingly demand accountability.
Institutional researchers, the data stewards for colleges and universities,
are becoming involved in such strategic planning, supporting efforts to
strengthen institutional efficiency and effectiveness in policymaking.
Researchers find that locating, preparing, and presenting necessary data
and information for planners is a challenging exercise. In this volume of *New
Directions for Institutional Research*, administrators, consultants, researchers,
and scholars provide unique, innovative approaches to that challenge. Some
authors introduce program applications and statistical techniques; others
share case studies. The variety of perspectives and depths of focus makes
this a timely, useful guide for institutional researchers.
ISBN: 978-04703-84534

IR136   Using Qualitative Methods in Institutional Assessment
Shaun R. Harper, Samuel D. Museus
This volume of *New Directions for Institutional Research* advocates the broad
use of qualitative methods in assessment across American higher education:
campus cultures, academic success and retention programs, student
experiences and learning, and teaching effectiveness. The chapter authors

suggest that responses to demands for increased accountability will be insufficient if researchers continue to rely almost exclusively on statistical analyses to assess institutional effectiveness. Instead, they recommend a variety of qualitative approaches that can produce rich and instructive data to guide institutional decision-making and action. In addition, they dispel common myths and misconceptions regarding the use of qualitative methods in assessment.
ISBN: 978-04702-83615

IR135 **Space: The Final Frontier for Institutional Research**
Nicholas A. Valcik
Facilities information, once a world of precious drawings and laborious calculations, has been transformed by the power of information technology. Blueprints securely locked in cabinets have given way to online systems based on geospatial information systems (GIS). The result is nimble systems adaptable to purposes across administrations, applications that integrate divisions—business, institutional research, student affairs—with shared information. This volume of *New Directions for Institutional Research* delves into this new world of facilities information. The authors show how to gather data and how state and other agencies use it. They discuss the necessity of accurate, accessible information for determining and apportioning indirect costs. They look at its use for student recruitment and retention, and they demonstrate how it can even be used to correlate various classroom attributes with student learning success. With twenty-first-century technology, facilities data is useful far beyond traditional business affairs operations—it has become integral to institutional planning and operation.
ISBN: 978-04702-55254

IR134 **Advancing Sustainability in Higher Education**
Larry H. Litten, Dawn Geronimo Terkla
Effective organizations strive constantly to improve. Colleges and universities are becoming increasingly aware of financial, social, and environmental challenges—both to their continued well-being and to the societies they serve—many of which are subsumed under the category of sustainability. In order to maintain progress, manage risk, and conserve resources, policymakers and managers need information that monitors performance, illuminates risk, and demonstrates responsible institutional behavior. Institutional researchers bring distinctive knowledge and skills to the table. This volume of *New Directions for Institutional Research* identifies various obstacles to sustainable progress and describes solutions for advancing educational institutions and the societies in which they are embedded.
ISBN: 978-04701-76870

IR133 **Using Quantitative Data to Answer Critical Questions**
Frances K. Stage
This volume of *New Directions for Institutional Research* challenges quantitative researchers to become more critical. By providing examples from the work of several prominent researchers, and by offering concrete recommendations, the editor and authors deliver messages that are likely to cause many educational researchers to reexamine their own work. The collective efforts described here will help readers become more sensitive to the nuances among various educational groups, and to pay more attention to outliers. This volume supplies both motivation and analytical support to those who might incorporate criticality into their own quantitative work, as well as to those who wish to read critical perspectives with an open mind about what they might find.
ISBN: 978-07879-97786

IR132   **Applying Economics to Institutional Research**
Robert K. Toutkoushian, Michael B. Paulsen
In many ways, economic concepts, models, and methods can be applied to
higher education research. This volume's chapter authors are all higher
education researchers with graduate training in economics and extensive
experience in institutional research. They share insight on the economist's
perspective of education costs and revenues, plus how to use economics to
inform enrollment management and to understand faculty labor market
issues.
ISBN: 978-07879-95768

IR131   **Data Mining in Action: Case Studies of Enrollment Management**
Jing Luan, Chun-Mei Zhao
Data mining has great potential to enhance institutional research. Six
case studies in this volume employed data mining for solving real-world
prob-lems in enrollment yield, retention, transfer-outs, utilization of
advanced-placement scores, predicting graduation rates, and more.
Discusses data mining vs. traditional statistics, debunks the myths, and
highlights the need for individual pattern recognition and customized
treatment of students.
ISBN: 0-7879-9426-X

IR130   **Reframing Persistence Research to Improve Academic Success**
Edward P. St. John, Michael Wilkerson
This volume proposes and tests new collaborations between institutional
researchers and others on campus who are engaged in breaking down
barriers to academic success, especially for minorities and nontraditional
students. What if traditional recommendations aren't effective? Chapters
review prior research and best practices, then investigate new approaches to
assessment, action research, action inquiry, and evaluation. Lessons learned
can inform strategies of administrators, faculty, and everyone interested in
improving success for all students.
ISBN: 0-7879-8759-X

IR129   **Analyzing Faculty Work and Rewards: Using Boyer's Four Domains of
Scholarship**
John M. Braxton
Boyer's four domains—scholarships of discovery, application, integration, and
teaching—influence and define scholars as their professional roles, career
stages, and research goals change. This volume offers practical suggestions for
academic reward structure, graduate school preparation, and state policy.
ISBN: 0-7879-8674-7

IR128   **Workforce Development and Higher Education: A Strategic Role for
Institutional Research**
Richard A. Voorhees, Lee Harvey
Workforce development is a growing area for higher education. This volume
examines its conceptual underpinnings from an international perspective, and
it provides practical institutional case studies and specific techniques for
gauging the market potential for new instructional programs. It discusses
suggested projects and studies for IR personnel to consider on their campuses.
ISBN: 0-7879-8365-9

NEW DIRECTIONS FOR INSTITUTIONAL RESEARCH

ORDER FORM SUBSCRIPTION AND SINGLE ISSUES

DISCOUNTED BACK ISSUES:

Use this form to receive 20% off all back issues of *New Directions for Institutional Research*.
All single issues priced at **$23.20** (normally $29.00)

TITLE	ISSUE NO.	ISBN

Call 888-378-2537 or see mailing instructions below. When calling, mention the promotional code JBXND
to receive your discount. For a complete list of issues, please visit www.josseybass.com/go/ndir

SUBSCRIPTIONS: (1 YEAR, 4 ISSUES)

☐ New Order   ☐ Renewal

U.S.	☐ Individual: $109	☐ Institutional: $264
CANADA/MEXICO	☐ Individual: $109	☐ Institutional: $304
ALL OTHERS	☐ Individual: $133	☐ Institutional: $338

Call 888-378-2537 or see mailing and pricing instructions below.
Online subscriptions are available at www.interscience.wiley.com

ORDER TOTALS:

Issue / Subscription Amount: $ _____

Shipping Amount: $ _____
(for single issues only – subscription prices include shipping)

Total Amount: $ _____

SHIPPING CHARGES:

SURFACE	DOMESTIC	CANADIAN
First Item	$5.00	$6.00
Each Add'l Item	$3.00	$1.50

(No sales tax for U.S. subscriptions. Canadian residents, add GST for subscription orders. Individual rate subscriptions must
be paid by personal check or credit card. Individual rate subscriptions may not be resold as library copies.)

BILLING & SHIPPING INFORMATION:

☐ **PAYMENT ENCLOSED:** *(U.S. check or money order only. All payments must be in U.S. dollars.)*

☐ **CREDIT CARD:**   ☐ VISA   ☐ MC   ☐ AMEX

Card number _____ Exp. Date _____

Card Holder Name _____ Card Issue # *(required)* _____

Signature _____ Day Phone _____

☐ **BILL ME:** *(U.S. institutional orders only. Purchase order required.)*

Purchase order # _____
Federal Tax ID 13559302 • GST 89102-8052

Name _____

Address _____

Phone _____ E-mail _____

Copy or detach page and send to: **John Wiley & Sons, PTSC, 5th Floor**
989 Market Street, San Francisco, CA 94103-1741

Order Form can also be faxed to: **888-481-2665**

PROMO JBXND